THE MAN TRANSLATOR

THE MAN TRANSLATOR

YOUR ESSENTIAL GUIDE TO MANLAND

ALISON GRAMBS

CITADEL PRESS
Kensington Publishing Corp.
www.kensingtonbooks.com

CITADEL PRESS BOOKS are published by

Kensington Publishing Corp.
850 Third Avenue
New York, NY 10022

Copyright © 2008 Alison Grambs

All Kensington titles, imprints, and distributed lines are available at special quantity discounts for bulk purchases for sales promotions, premiums, fund-raising, educational, or institutional use. Special book excerpts or customized printings can also be created to fit specific needs. For details, write or phone the office of the Kensington special sales manager: Kensington Publishing Corp., 850 Third Avenue, New York, NY 10022, attn: Special Sales Department; phone 1-800-221-2647.

CITADEL PRESS and the Citadel logo are Reg. U.S. Pat. & TM Off.

First printing: January 2008

10 9 8 7 6 5 4 3 2 1

Printed in the United States of America

Library of Congress Control Number: 2007937041

ISBN 13: 978-0-8065-2859-5
ISBN 10: 0-8065-2859-1

To Mom, Dad, and Tommy,
who make the journey to anyplace feel safe.

Contents

Manland: National Statistics

National Flower: Poison Ivy

Name for Inhabitants: Man, Butthead, Jackass, A-hole, Bud, Dude, Bro, Guy, Yo!

National motto: "Huh?"

First settler: Adam

National threat: Woman

National ally: Dog

Natural resource: Gas

Population: A lot.

National climate: (see Weather Forecasting in Manland, page 13)

Average IQ: Depends on Man's sobriety

National dish: Pizza

National beverage: Beer

National sporting activity: Anything that involves grunting, sweating, and broken limbs.

National tribal wear: Pit-stained T-shirt circa 1990, sweatpants that used to be gray, but are now light black, and sneakers that used to be white, but are now gray.

National pasttime: Any sport that can be observed from the sofa.

Country nickname: No Man's Land.

Preferred form of exercise: Masturbation

National industry: Beer bellies

Introduction

The cool thing about being famous is traveling. I have always wanted to travel across seas, like to Canada and stuff.

—Britney Spears

Whenever you travel to a foreign country you inevitably pack the essentials: a passport, some traveler's checks, toiletries, decent walking shoes, and several pairs of clean underwear (one would hope). But more important to have on your person than anything else is a pocket travel guide. For whether you are flying to Paris to spit off the Eiffel Tower, or cruising to Greece to graffiti your name on the Parthenon, your travel guide enables you to achieve maximum cultural absorption and suffer minimal public embarrassment.

With the mere flip of a page you learn how to ask a Roman gladiator where the bathroom is at the Coliseum, and more important, understand the answer so you don't pee in the wrong place. A travel guide preps you on the way to order dinner in India, so you get the chilled monkey brains only if you actually *want* the chilled monkey brains. A travel guide advises you of important national holidays to observe while sipping tea with the Queen in England, alerts you to cultural customs you must respect while camel racing in Egypt, and clues you in to the difference between the Walk and Do Not Walk signs in China so you don't get run over by six billion people pedaling around on bicycles.

In other words, a travel guide makes your trip to a foreign country feel, well, not quite so foreign. And amazingly, from South Africa to the North Pole, from Australia to some godforsaken dot on the globe called Tuvalu, there is a handbook out there for pretty much every exotic destination imaginable. Except one: the most frightening, mysterious and dangerous country of all.

Manland.

Yes, for centuries women have been expected to navigate their way through the vexing jungle of the male species without so much as a compass to guide them. We have lost our minds trying to understand the male heart, the male psyche, male body language, and male dating customs. Been left to hazard mere guesses as to what makes Man happy and what makes him sad. What it means when Man takes you to a roadside hot dog truck on your first date. What deep emotions Man is trying to express when he passes gas. Or what Man means when he says, "I love you" while scratching his balls.

Fear not. Help is finally here. From translating the convoluted language of Manspeak to deciphering the meaning of Man's every gesture, facial expression, and grunting noise, this book demystifies the testicle-bearing gender once and for all. Now you will know exactly what to expect when dealing with this beast who eats stale pizza for breakfast and considers the television remote an appendage. All of the strange rituals of the male world are finally exposed! The bizarre traditions. The seemingly illogical patterns of behavior. The backwards system of communication and expression. At last, there are no more secrets, ladies! You are about to learn what makes Man tick, and what ticks Man off. Everything you need to know about this disturbing, and slightly dimwitted, creature is right here in this book.

So, fasten your seat belt, and get ready for the most important trip you will ever take. We hope you enjoy your stay in Manland . . . or, at the very least survive it. Girl, it may be a Man's world out there . . . but now you won't be quite so lost in it.

THE MAN
TRANSLATOR

CHAPTER ONE

Before Your Departure

A journey of a thousand miles must begin
with a single step.

—Lao Tzu

So, you've cleared some vacation days with your boss, purchased your ticket, and are finally on your way to Manland. Whether it's a day trip, a weekend jaunt, or a permanent vacation, you are raring to go. But before you board that proverbial plane into the jungle that is the male habitat there are a few things you need to take care of.

To-Do List

1. Notify your loved ones that you are leaving on a life-threatening trip, so they can send out a search party if you don't return.
2. Toss out all house plants. Better you mercy kill them, than leave them to die of neglect.
3. Make sure the dog and cat have food. (Make sure you have a dog and cat first, of course.)

4. Leave a sign on your front door that reads, "Dear Burglars, I am away. Please stay out. Thanks!"
5. Erase all old messages from your mother on your answering machine to make room for all the annoying "Oh, heavens to Betsy! Why haven't you returned my calls? Are you all right? I'm calling the police . . ." messages she will leave while you are gone.

Travel Tips: *Check Your Baggage*

By nature Man is an uncomplicated creature, and he likes Woman to be the same. So, when entering into a new relationship in Manland, it is vital that you check your baggage at the door, so to speak. Man lives in the present. He is not interested in your past. As a matter of fact, he wishes you didn't have one.

Travel Essentials

Getting to Manland is all well and good, but arriving there fully prepared is crucial to your survival. Just as with any other excursion, you simply must have all the basic essentials with you. You know, those little creature comforts that can mean the difference between having the best trip of your life and the worst vacation ever. So, make sure you have the following in your luggage:

Packing Checklist

1. Hand sanitizer
2. A case of Lysol
3. Condoms
4. Clean underwear
5. A yoga mat and whatever meditative mantra you employ when you feel yourself going insane
6. Bottle of extra-strength headache medicine
7. Disposable toilet seat covers
8. Emergency cash for that emergency cab ride home when things go terribly wrong
9. A photo ID (the real one, not the one that says you're eighteen . . . or a "natural" blonde)
10. Hairspray to make your hair look bigger (and thus more intimidating)
11. Extra cover-up stick because those bags under your eyes aren't going to conceal themselves
12. Breath freshener (yes, you *do* need it)
13. A fully charged cell phone with 911, your shrink, and your mommy all on speed dial
14. Shoes with short heels for when you need to make a quick escape, and shoes with high heels for when you're going for that whore look
15. Disposable razors
16. Any and all feminine hygiene products you may require during your stay, but with the names of said products blacked out for privacy purposes (Especially that box of stuff you have for that unspeakable itch in that unspeakable place)

"Man-tras"

In case of an emergency, it is essential that you have a few important meditative forces on your side. Review the following Man-Tras. Commit them to memory. Any time you feel yourself getting flustered on your journey into Manland, find a quiet (and reasonably clean) place to sit down, cross your legs, and recite the following. These can save your life. Or at the very least, keep you from being institutionalized.

1. Man is just like a woman . . . only with smaller breasts and more facial hair.
2. When in doubt, assume Man's brain is not functioning at full capacity.
3. Anything is edible with some ketchup on it.
4. *Clean* is a relative term.
5. What happens in Manland, stays in Manland . . . unless I was stupid enough to take photographs, in which case, I'm screwed.
6. You can lead Man away from the television set, but you cannot make him turn it off.
7. Pencillin cures everything.
8. A Man is only as good as his word . . . or his credit score.
9. All Men are created equal . . . equally stupid, that is.
10. I can always become a lesbian.

The Origin of Man

In order to understand Man, you must first understand how Man came to be . . . the putz that he is.

There are two theories as to the beginnings of Man's existence. Subscribe to whichever one speaks to you spiritually. Or whichever one simply takes less time to read. Your choice.

The Creation Theory

ON THE SEVENTH DAY OF THE FIRST WEEK in history God created the Garden of Eden which, by the way, was located where present-day Las Vegas is. At first, the place wasn't much to look at. So, God added some nice foliage, a couple of fluffy animals, a giant waterfall, a canyon, and a few rock formations here and there. Nice enough. But something was missing. There was no one to enjoy the Garden (or trim the hedges).

So, God created Man. He picked up a ball of dust he spied lying on the ground, performed some sort of CPR-like move on it, and magically breathed life into an odd-looking creature with a furry back and receding hairline. God named this creature "Adam," though truth be told, Adam actually looked more like a "Chuck." However, much to God's disappointment, Adam/Chuck didn't really do much once he was created. He just moped around in the Garden day and night, muttering to himself because there was no cable television or Doritos. He refused to put on clothes, arguing that boxers didn't give him "enough support," and briefs made him feel "restricted." And Man never remembered to water the ficus plants. He left litter all over the Garden and did not mow the lawn once. What's worse? He was constantly touching himself in his private place in public.

5

It wasn't long before God realized he had screwed up big time. Clearly, Adam/Chuck was incapable of functioning by himself. He was a body without the brain. And already feeling pangs of guilt for creating the completely illogical platypus, God worked hard to correct his mistake. He knocked Adam/Chuck unconscious, removed one of his ribs and, with that rib, fashioned a new and improved version of Man: Woman. God named this beautiful and perfect creature Eve, though truth be told, she looked more like a Petula. He presented Eve/Petula to Adam/Chuck who, ever the deep thinker, remarked, "*Yowza! She's hot!*" Eve/Petula taught Adam/Chuck how to talk, think, turn a fig leaf into haute couture, reheat leftovers—that sort of thing. She even managed to spruce up the Garden of Eden until it was looking so refined it was featured on the cover of *Only Home & Garden* magazine.

And so Adam/Chuck and Eve/Petula lived happily ever after. (Until, of course, that unfortunate serpent-and-the-apple incident . . . but why focus on the negative, right?)

The Evolution Theory

A LONG, LONG TIME AGO, before the advent of fire or the cordless telephone, two warring clans of monkeys roamed the Earth: the Us clan and the Them clan. The Us-es were a mean bunch of monkeys who disrespected the land and left their banana peels all over the place; and the Thems eventually got so tired of the abuse they declared war on the Us-es. After all, the future of monkeys was at stake. The battle was bloody and vicious, and, in the first few rounds, it looked as though the Thems were about to be obliterated. But then a spectator who was watching the fight, a particularly bright female member of the Thems, named Tallulah, shouted at the top of her lungs from the bleachers,

"Hey, idiots. Why don't you guys try walking upright? You'll be able to fight much better with your hands free."

One by one, the Them chimps balanced on their hindquarters and stood upright. The Us chimps scoffed at these silly-looking chimps and the silly manner in which they were fighting, and continued to fight on all fours. But the Thems had the last laugh as they soon beat the Us clan in the great battle and returned home heroes. To celebrate, the soldier chimps headed down to the local watering hole for a night of drunken banana peeling.

Once again, Tallulah, who was bartending part time to pay for chiropractic school, was disturbed by the stupidity exhibited by her fellow monkeys. She couldn't help but feel sorry for the suckers as they struggled to peel their celebratory bananas with their teeth and crack open their celebratory beer cans on rocks. Once again, she shouted at the fools.

"Hey, idiots! Why don't you boys use your opposable thumbs to peel those bananas and open those cans? It'll save you a lot of time."

Once again, the Us clan members scoffed at such an absurd suggestion. And once again, they were proven wrong for now the Homo erecti (as they mockingly called the Thems), could not only open beer cans, but hitchhike, macramé jungle vines into fabulous necklace and bracelet sets, not to mention play chess. But the Homo erecti's victory was short-lived for, one day, the planet was overcome by a massive heat wave. Suffering beneath their thick layers of fur, all the monkeys in the land began dropping like flies from heat stroke. Once again, Dr. Tallulah (she was now a licensed chiropractor) saved the day.

"Hey, idiots. Why don't you use the sharp edge of that rock over there to shave off all your body fur. That'll cool you off." (Waxing salons weren't invented until the Pleistocene era.)

Of course, the Us clan monkeys scoffed at this silly idea, and eventually started dying of dehydration. But the Homo erecti had learned that Dr. Tallulah knew of what she squawked. Away went their tufts of bothersome arm hair, the itchy foot hair, the shoulder hair, the back hair! Now, with their smooth, cool skin, and their multifunctional thumbs and sexy walks, the Homo erecti were the chimps to beat. They became total ladies' men, and advanced socially and intellectually—driving convertible cars, organizing high-end-stakes fantasy football games, attending college, and working on Wall Street. Yes, eventually, the Homo erecti evolved into modern Man.

And whatever became of those snickering little Us monkeys who didn't listen to Dr. Tallulah? Well, they got locked up in zoos . . . or cast in really bad television sitcoms.

CHAPTER TWO
Cultural Notes

*If you reject the food, ignore the customs,
fear the religion, and avoid the people, you
might better stay at home.*

—James A. Michener

You've heard the saying, "When in Rome, do as the Romans do." Well, hardly does this adage give you license to go about doing *everything* the Romans did. Frankly, they weren't the most stable of people—what with declaring horses senators, and tossing Christians to the lions. But overall, it is a good rule of thumb by which to travel.

So, just as you should be aware of the major Australian bank holidays when planning a jaunt Down Under, and take note of particular tribal customs when organizing your romp into the Amazon, it is wise to acquaint yourself with male "culture" and customs when journeying into Manland. After all, the more you know about your host country, the better you can blend in. And the more you blend in, the less likely you are to make a fool of yourself and embarrass the rest of us.

So, let's learn the basic facts about Manland, shall we?

Dates, Times, and Seasons in Manland

An important part of assimilating into the culture of Manland is understanding its unique system of dates, times, seasons, and holidays. As you might expect, it can be a bit complex and illogical, so don't worry if you can't master it right away.

Days of the Week

Man takes his week quite seriously.

While the days of the week in Manland may *sound* the same as our days of the week, the difference is that the Manland week revolves entirely around Monday Night Football, an event akin to the high holy days celebrated in other, more normal countries. Now, as frustrating as this code may be to grasp, Man's weekly calendar is not to be questioned or revised in any way by tourists or visitors. Unlike Woman, Man cannot think outside the Pigskin Box.

Monday: Monday Night Football Day
Tuesday: Six days until Monday Night Football
Wednesday: Five days until Monday Night Football
Thursday: Four days until Monday Night Football
Friday: Three days until Monday Night Football
Saturday: Two days until Monday Night Football
Sunday: One day until Monday Night Football

Months of the Year

While Woman distinguishes the months of the year by selflessly associating them with important holidays celebrating the good deeds of our forefathers or noteworthy birthdays of those in her charge, the Manland calendar is a bit more egocentric.

January: The month Man growls at his credit card bill from the holiday season preceding.

February: The month Man buys you a bunch of Valentine's Day gifts you don't want and can't return because he lost the receipts.

March: The month Man pretends he is Irish so he has an excuse to stumble around drunk off his butt for twenty-four hours.

April: The month Man finds, and then consumes, all of the Easter eggs you hid for the children.

May: The month Man is forced to remember to buy his mother flowers.

June: The month Man buys his father the same tie he's been buying him since Man was six years old.

July: The month Man inevitably blows off the tip of his finger playing with fireworks.

August: The month Man's armpits stink to high heaven even though he showered.

September: The month Man begins talking about the Super Bowl, even though it is still several months away.

October: The month Man uses as an excuse to dress up like Woman and beg for candy from strangers.

November: The month in which Man devotes all of his attention to a turkey dinner and the Dallas Cowboys kickoff schedule.

December: The month Man insists on decorating the entire house with Christmas lights and giant reindeer statues.

Important Manland Dates to Remember

In Manland, the inhabitants, both young and old, are shaped by these important dates in history.

February 6, 1895: Babe Ruth is born.

August 5, 1960: The American government approves the birth-control pill.

July 1, 1967: Pamela Anderson is born.

January 12, 1969: Joe Namath guarantees victory as an 18-point underdog in Super Bowl and wins.

September 21, 1970: Monday Night Football is born.

February 22, 1980: The USA Hockey Team defeats Soviet Union in Olympics.

August 23, 1989: Pete Rose is banned from baseball.

October 15, 1989: Wayne Gretzky becomes the NHL's all-time leading scorer.

September 14, 1994: The World Series is canceled.

February 19, 1995: Pamela Anderson and Tommy Lee marry.

September 1, 1995: The Sony Playstation is released in the U.S.

April 1997: Pamela Anderson and Tommy Lee's sex video is released to the public.

June 28, 1997: Mike Tyson bites Evander Holyfield's ear.

April 1999: Pamela Anderson has her breast implants removed.

October 26, 2000: The Sony Playstation2 is released in the U.S.

February 1, 2004: Janet Jackson exposes her nipple at Super Bowl XXXVIII.

October 28, 2004: The Boston Red Sox win their first World Series since 1918.

March 4, 2005: The Sony PSP is released in the U.S.
July 29, 2006: Pamela Anderson marries Kid Rock.
November 27, 2006: Pamela Anderson divorces Kid Rock.
June 3, 2007: Paris Hilton goes to jail.
June 7, 2007: Paris Hilton is released from jail.
June 13, 2007: Paris Hilton is sent back to jail.

Weather Forecasting in Manland

The weather in Manland can be unpredictable, depending on the time of year and location of your visit. It can also be difficult to analyze, as Man has a bizarre way of communicating the forecast. He doesn't just say the logical, "it's hot" or "it's cold." Instead, Man personalizes the weather. So, if you want to know whether or not to bring an umbrella on your stroll you need to know how to interpret the weather report in Manland.

Man says: "Hey, nice nipples, honey!"
Forecast: "It's a bit nippy out there, so bundle up."

The Four Seasons in Manland

Baseball season
Hockey season
Football season
Basketball season

Man says: "My pits stink."
Translation: "It is rather humid."

Telling Time in Manland

Below is an example of common dialogue concerning time in Manland. You are likely to hear this in both formal and casual situations:
You ask: "What time is it?"
Man responds: "I dunno. Look at the clock."

Man says: "Damn. The baseball game is gonna be canceled."
Translation: "High levels of precipitation are indicating a likely chance of rain."

Man says: "You're gonna look stupid in that jacket."
Translation: "It's unseasonably warm today."

Man says: "You should use extra hairspray."
Translation: "Strong winds are coming in from the north."

Man says: "Holy crap! My pee froze in midstream."
Translation: "Arctic temperatures have moved in and temperatures have fallen below zero."

Man says: "I need to put chains on the car."
Translation: "It's snowing."

Man says: "My ball sac's shriveled up."
Translation: "It is quite chilly out there."

Man says: "My ass is sweating—need to change my underwear."

Translation: "There is a heat stroke advisory for the surrounding counties."

Man says: "You shouldn't wear mascara today."
Translation: "Rain showers are expected all day."

Currency and Cost of Travel

Fortunately for budget travelers, money is not the preferred currency in Manland. Instead, the citizens of Manland have developed a complex system of exchange in order to better suit the needs of their society. Please see the list below for common bartering details.

What you want: A foot massage
What it costs: A beer in a frosted glass, hand delivered

What you want: Man to take out the trash
What it costs: Flash your boobies once

What you want: Man to take out the trash without complaining
What it costs: Flash your boobies twice

What you want: A full body massage
What it costs: A full hour of complete silence

What you want: Man to walk the dog
What it costs: You swap out your little rat dog for a German shepherd

What you want: Man to load the dishwasher
What it costs: Tickets to a local football game

What you want: Man to drive your mother to the airport
What it costs: Tickets to the Super Bowl

What you want: Man to cancel poker night
What it costs: Sex without cuddling afterward

What you want: Man to watch a chick flick with you
What it costs: A year's subscription to *Maxim* magazine

What you want: Man to go grocery shopping with you
What it costs: Man gets to choose the food and eat it while
  he keeps you company in the aisles

What you want: Man to pick up tampons for you
What it costs: You not using PMS to your advantage for a
  month

What you want: Man to stop acting like an idiot
What it costs: You stop nagging him for five minutes

What you want: Man to throw out all his porno tapes
What it costs: You start doing everything that chick in the
  porno tapes does

What you want: Man to stop snoring
What it costs: You stop stealing the covers

What you want: Man to do the laundry
What it costs: You fold

What you want: Man to talk about his feelings
What it costs: You don't talk about yours

What you want: Man to put the toilet seat down
What it costs: You take up pole dancing

The Metric System in Manland

As you may have noticed by now, everything in Manland is different. The Manland metric system is no exception.

1 regular inch = 2.6 Man inches (wink, wink)

Not unlike the weight system commonly used by Woman:

1 regular pound = .5 Woman pounds
(wink, wink)

Driving in Manland

Driving the vast country of Manland can be quite an exciting experience, but you should proceed with caution. Though it is widely known that female drivers are far superior to males, the backward culture of Manland has yet to acknowledge this fact, thus resulting in unfair scrutiny and ridicule of the manner in which a female operates a motor vehicle. Protect yourself by understanding some of the basic principles of driving in Manland.

Road Signs and What They Mean in Manland

Just as the English drive on the wrong side of the street . . . from the wrong side of the car . . . nothing Man does behind the wheel makes sense. He drives by his own rules, interpreting traffic signs merely to suit his needs. So, for Woman in Manland, driving isn't a privilege—it's a near-death experience.

 STOP: Slow down for a second, then keep going.

 NO U-TURN: Check to see if a cop is around. If not, go ahead and make an illegal U-turn.

 YIELD: Maintain speed, but be aware someone may crash into you.

 MERGE: Speed into the oncoming lane and pray for the best.

 NO RIGHT ON RED: Check for cops, then make the right.

 PEDESTRIAN CROSSING: Maintain speed, but swerve to avoid hitting pedestrians.

 SPEED LIMIT 65 MPH: Suggested speed limit, but see if you can do more without getting a ticket.

NO PASSING: Pass as long as you've got two inches clearance and a reasonably good shot at not getting killed.

 GAS STATION AHEAD: Ignore and do not pull over, no matter how close to Empty you are.

 NO ENTRY: Screw it—go.

 NO PARKING: Curse, spit, and give the finger to sign. Then pull away and burn rubber.

 SLIPPERY WHEN WET: Step on the gas.

 MOOSE CROSSING: Aim for moose at high velocity.

 RED LIGHT: Keep going through it, and howl a line from *Smokey and the Bandit*.

Manland Cars and What They Mean

In some cultures, they say the eyes are the window to the soul. In Manland, it is often said that the car is the window to the soul. You can tell a lot about Man from the automobile he drives. Below is a list of some of the most common personalities behind the cars.

Candy-apple-red sports car: "I have a small penis, and an even smaller brain."

Convertible: "I am carefree, and this is totally my own hair."

Open-top Jeep: "I am an all-American dude who knows how to kill."

Hybrid: "I am environmentally aware, and possibly gay."

Compact SUV: "I can't afford a real SUV."

Minivan: "I have twenty kids and a fat wife."

Pickup truck with a gun rack: "I'm looking to settle down with one of my cousins and live off the land."

Giant SUV: "I don't give a crap about the environment and can't park this thing for the life of me."

Station wagon: "I am ninety years old and partially senile."

Motorcycle: "During the week, I'm an accountant, but on the weekends, I'm a Hell's Angel"

Scooter: "I can't handle a motorcycle, but am banking on the fact that some chicks can't tell the difference."

Bicycle: "I have no money, but great hamstring muscles."

Driving with Man

If you are unfortunate enough to end up in the passenger seat while doing a vehicular tour of Manland, there are a few key rules of procedure you must follow. Man's car is his baby. And just as you would be insane to interfere with a lioness's cub while on safari in Africa, you are taking your life into your own hands if you mess with Man's car. He *lives* for his car. And will kill whoever so much as touches his cup holders.

1. If you are driving with Man and he becomes lost, you will notice his reluctance to do the obvious: stop and ask for directions. When this happens, pretend you have to go to the bathroom and have him pull into the nearest

gas station. While Man is under the assumption you are merely using the facilities, sneak into the food mart and ask the cashier for directions.

2. Do not, under any circumstance, store your lipstick in Man's glove compartment when on a road trip. It will inevitably melt all over some stupid knickknack Man has kept in there since 1987 and he will whine and cry for the rest of the trip.

3. Whenever you switch from the driver's seat to the passenger seat make sure to return the driver's seat to Man's preferred position. Man cannot handle change, and will freak out if he suddenly finds his legs all bent and the steering wheel pressed up against his chest.

4. Whatever you do, do not . . . we repeat, *do not*, change the settings on the radio.

6. As a general rule of thumb, Man will roll all the car windows down when it is freezing outside, and roll them all up when the whole land is suffering from a massive heat wave and the car air conditioning on the fritz. All you can do to maintain a safe body temperature is always travel with a sweater and a bag of ice.

5. Though practicality would suggest otherwise, apparently the rearview mirror is not for touching up your makeup. Use the one supplied in the visor in front of your seat. It'll cause fewer fights—and accidents.

Driving Body Language

Much like a chimpanzee, Man conveys his mood not only via a series of grunting noises, but through body language. Knowing how to read between the lines when Man is behind the wheel will save you a lot of headaches.

Physical Gesture	Meaning
One hand on steering wheel	Man is freeing up his other hand for the occasional nose pick.
Both hands on steering wheel	Man had one too many beers and is desperately trying to stay in between the white lines.
One arm out the window	Man has farted and is trying to air it out.
Pointing middle finger at passing drivers	Man is not in a sociable mood.
Continually looking in his rearview mirror	Man has either violated a traffic law and is being pursued by the cops . . . or there is a hot woman in a convertible driving behind him.

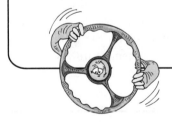

Occupational Hazards

Manland offers a wide array of jobs, ranging from professional to blue collar. But beware of the hidden meanings behind even the most prestigious-sounding job: In Manland, nothing is as it seems. Much is revealed by the career path Man has chosen. Information is power, ladies—power to know when to give Man your phone number . . . and when to run like the wind.

Accountant: Not the most exciting of conversationalists, but very handy to have around come tax season.

Actor: Temperamental, insecure, and egotistical . . . but can get you a great discount if you show up during his shift at TGI Fridays.

Architect: Detail-oriented, nostalgic, and obsessed with measuring everything.

Attorney: Wealthy, intelligent, and totally impossible to win an argument with.

Ballet dancer: Highly flexible, but prone to trying on your clothes when you're not home.

Banker: Always has cash in his wallet, but suffers from an unnatural fear of ski masks.

Bus driver: Can get you across town in no time, but is addicted to hemorrhoid cream.

Chef: Cooks you fabulous meals for breakfast, lunch, and dinner, but always reeks of garlic.

Computer technician: Looks like a major dweeb, and spends his days fiddling with hard drives and motherboards, but he's got some serious byte.

Construction worker: Has a body to die for and can whistle really well.

Dentist: Enjoys causing other people pain, but has made it socially acceptable to wear white after Labor Day.

Dog walker: Wonderful with animals, but has trouble relating to people unless they are wearing a collar and leash.

Fast-food server: Suffers from abominable acne, but can get you free fries anytime you want them.

Firefighter: Incredibly strong, virile, and brave—and a huge fan of barbecue food.

Flight attendant: Gay . . . don't even bother.

Glassblower: Very popular with flight attendants.

Interior decorator: A great observer of color and texture, and wonderfully skilled at spending other people's money.

Mailman: The first person to see the new *Sports Illustrated* swimsuit edition, and the last person who should be wearing shorts in public.

Massage therapist: Very touchy feely, and pretty much a borderline male prostitute.

Mobster: Can get you a great deal on a "retail" fur coat . . . but only if he actually lives to see tomorrow.

Model: Can tell you his name, but probably can't spell it.

Mortician: Soft-spoken, and a bit depressing to be around . . . but can offer you some wonderful makeup suggestions.

Museum security guard: Will invite you over to his place, but yell at you if you touch any of his knickknacks.

Musician: Will provide you with endlessly fascinating discourse on the history of jazz over a meal . . . he just can't afford to pay for that meal.

Novelist: A raging alcoholic, but knows what a semicolon is . . . and more important, how to use it correctly!

Nurse: Has a wonderful bedside manner but is obsessed with bedpans.

Personal trainer: Has a great body, and likes to bench press you for fun.

Plumber: Can unclog any part of a Woman, but will do it with his butt crack showing.

Police officer: Risks his life to protect his fellow citizens . . . unless there is a glazed pastry around to nibble on.

Politician: Out to make the world a better place . . . (and if you believe that crap, we've also got a bridge to sell ya!)

Priest: (Sorry, not available . . . so just move on.)

Proctologist: Medically knowledgeable, but works with a lot of asses.

Professional athlete: Rich, spoiled, and willing to endorse anything.

Professional war re-enactor: Lives in the past and has a penchant for burlap underwear.

Pilot: Looks great in a uniform and is definitely a member of the Mile High Club.

Real estate agent: Knows all the best neighborhoods and would sell his mother for a 3 percent commission.

Used car salesman: Lies through his teeth about everything, but can get you a great deal on a 1975 Volkswagen.

Shrink: A complete nutcase who makes his living convincing everyone else they're crazy.

Surgeon: Has the personality of a thumbtack, but is great to have around to carve the turkey on Thanksgiving.

Teacher: Smart, patient, and always has a number 2 pencil on hand.

Vineyard owner: Has exquisite taste, but can't pass a breathalyzer test to save his life.

Manland Sightseeing Itinerary

Now that you know what kind of creatures you are likely to encounter in Manland, it's time to observe them in their natural habitat. Fortunately there are myriad places a tourist can perch herself in this vast countryside to observe the inhabitants in their natural surroundings. Though it can be dangerous, if you study Man in any of these suggested areas, you will get a true glimpse of how this testosterone-producing creature lives, and thus will be better prepared for any future encounters. Just bring some disinfectant with you, as many of these Manland territories can be hazardous to your health.

1. *The Bathroom:* The Manland bathroom is a scientist's wet dream. A bevy of bodily fluid samples, single-cell organisms, and remnants of personal hygiene products miraculously coexist in this petri dish of a locale. And the sights and smells emanating from this place are unlike those found in any other region of the world.

   What to bring: In order to safely observe Man in this locale, you *must* wear protective gear, such as a full body condom, and equip yourself with a set of nose plugs, ear plugs, a can of Lysol, and a medical release form listing an emergency contact and your blood type in case you pass out and are admitted to the nearest hospital.

   What you will see: Many a fascinating thing occurs in the Manland bathroom. Not only is this where Man washes, dries, shaves, primps, and releases his bowels, but it is also where he does most of his thinking. Some of the greatest minds in Manland history gave birth to their now famous theorems and logarithms in this very spot. If you're lucky, you may just bear witness to the next genius of our century during this tour. (Probably not, but a girl can dream.)

2. *The Strip Club:* A hot spot in the Manland red light district, this is where Man goes to enjoy mediocre food, watered-down drinks, bad music, and giant fake breasts. The clientele is strictly male, but the staff is always female (and often the victims of childhood neglect).

What to bring: Antibacterial hand sanitizer.

What you will see: This joint is where you are most likely to observe Man performing one of the basic male functions: humping. Humping the tables. Humping the chairs. Humping the waitresses. Humping the stage. Do not be afraid. This is completely normal behavior in this region of Manland. As a matter of fact—it's encouraged.

3. *A Super Bowl Party:* Ah, the Mecca of Manland. Observe Man at this event and you will bear witness to this gender's most primitive behavioral patterns. And seeing as it only comes once a year, we're talking really, really weird stuff going on.

What to bring: A cargo bin full of nachos, a case of beer, another case of beer, earplugs, a hat bearing the logo of the favored team, a hat bearing the logo of the unfavored team, cigars, a megaphone.

What you will see: This event brings out Man's most animalistic instincts. Leaping up and down on the couch.

Hurling wads of onion dip at the television set. Screaming at the little Man in the black-and-white-striped uniform on said TV. Farting, burping, weeping, cheering, and puking. Now doesn't that sound fun?

4. *The Gym:* This is where Man goes to bulk up . . . or give the appearance of bulking up . . . or watch members of the opposite sex watch Man bulking up.

   What to bring: A sports bra, a clean towel, and a bottle of water.

   What you will see: Man kissing his biceps. Man admiring his abs in the mirror. Man walking back and forth to the water cooler every five seconds. Man sweating all over the equipment and leaving his sweat there in a puddle for the next user to slip on. Man growling as he hoists more weight over his head than his trainer told him is safe to lift. Man screaming in pain when he realizes he made a mistake hoisting more weight over his head than his trainer told him was safe.

5. *The Office:* This is the habitat in which Man must perform specific tasks, based on his skill level, in exchange for a paycheck. This place does not make Man happy. It represents all that is wrong with his life. It is the place where Man is most likely to exhibit signs of stress and regret.

   What to bring: A paper shredder, a bottle of whiskey, a whoopee cushion.

   What you will see: Man writing things down. Typing at a keyboard. Pulling at his hair. Sighing loudly. Fighting with the copier. Talking to invisible people through a strange thing inserted in his ear. Pacing. Arguing. Attempting to grab at the breasts of the female office inhabitants.

Other Forms of Entertainment

If a tourist has some down time in London, she takes in a show in the city's West End. If she finds herself bored after days of touring the Coliseum and the rest of Rome's ancient ruins, she will head off to the opera house to enjoy the latest production of *La Traviata*. And the best way to get the most out of your stay in Manland is to go out and have some fun Man-style.

There is a bevy of entertainment events to enjoy during your stay in Manland. The citizens of this fun-filled country are enviably adept at occupying their free time. Their ability to find new and exciting ways to pass the days, months, and years away is simply unrivaled by any other nation. Some of them are organized forms of play that involve large crowds and expensive refreshment stands. And others are more homespun.

Live spectator events: Man enjoys entertainment options that not only cost exorbitant amounts of money, but enable him to watch something exciting happening from a seated position. Most of these take place in large stadiums or arenas. Here are a few of his favorites.

1. *Rock concerts:* Manland rock concerts are held in an arena that is often billowing with the smoke of various opiates. The music played at the concerts is anything involving loud screaming by the lead singer, lyrics that

don't really make sense, and about three very similar guitar riffs played over and over and over again with only the volume changing.

2. *Competitive contact sports:* These involve a bunch of overpaid, steroid-using citizens playing on two opposing teams. Said teams meet on a field, and then run around the field either throwing, catching, or chasing after a ball while the fans cheer and yell at them from the stands for about three hours.

3. *Mud wrestling:* This national pastime involves Man duping unsuspecting Women tourists into dressing themselves in string bikinis and rolling around each other in a pit filled with mud. Don't let this happen to you!

4. *"Professional" wrestling:* This is a sport in which extremely bulky Men gather in a large rubber-matted ring, wearing Women's underwear and slathered in oil. They then spend the next few hours stomping around the ring, falling around the ring, chasing each other around the ring, throwing each other across the ring, and throwing each other out of the ring. The winner is predetermined by whoever has the most endorsement deals for kids' cereal at the present time.

5. *Cock fights:* This one pretty much explains itself.

6. *NASCAR races:* This sporting event appeals mostly to those Men who hail from the southernmost region of Manland. Fans (usually all related) pay a lot of money to

gather at an outdoor racetrack and watch cars zoom around a track at about 200 miles per hour. A race is deemed exciting when at least one car crashes into the wall and bursts into flames.

Nonspectator events: Sometimes Man is a bit low on Manland currency and can't afford to attend public spectator events. In this case, Man can be rather enterprising, filling the empty space with creative pastimes that require nothing more than imagination. These are Man's favorite things to do when he has some free time on his hands:

1. *The basket shot:* An office-based sport that can be played either alone, or with some fellow citizens. It involves wadding up pieces of paper and aiming them at a trash receptacle on the other side of the room.

2. *Group urination:* This pastime usually takes place in the woods, on the roof of a building, or on a public street after the Manland bars have closed. Each Man unzips his pants, removes his reproductive organ from its sheath, and then proceeds to relieve himself. Sometimes the Men compete to see who can aim the farthest, or, if the Men are in a communal mood, they all attempt to cross their streams of pee and quote lines from the *Star Wars* films.

3. *Jerking off:* This is an activity that every Man engages in, no matter how much he denies it. Much like group urination, it involves removing one's reproductive organ from its sheath, but is performed while alone, in a private place (one would hope). Jerking off (also commonly

referred to as masturbation and choking the chicken) requires Man to conjure up images in his head of large-breasted Women with open mouths and expressions of willingness on their faces. Once those images have been established, Man fondles his nether region until his organ stands at attention. Then, when he feels his organ about to cough, he fondles it one last time until it releases a fluid into a nearby receptacle, such as a tissue, or sometimes Man's gym sock.

4. *Watching television:* This activity frequently involves Man lying on the sofa like a beached whale, staring glassy-eyed into a large box that projects moving images. This is a pastime Man tends to enjoy more than anything else but number 3. Actually, depending on what images are being projected on the large box, Man sometimes engages in number 3 while doing this one.

The Arts

If you're looking for even more sightseeing during your trip, look no further than the art of Manland. The Italians have da Vinci. The French have Cezanne. The Americans have Pollock. And Man has created a category of art that is all his own. Drawing heavily on influences from ancient cave drawings to animated motion pictures to modern sportscasters, Manland features a vibrant art scene that is unlike anything else on Earth. While you're in Manland, you may come across some of the following cutting-edge art:

1. Man's booger collection, which he keeps beneath the dining room table.
2. Pre-1985 posters of Farrah Fawcett.
3. Any "classic" car (i.e., hunk of junk) that's been sitting in the garage since the Reagan administration.
4. Chuck Norris movies.
5. Sports team logos.
6. Monster trucks.
7. Any film showing breasts, genitals, or Woman-on-Woman action.
8. A photograph of a NASCAR track. (See also: Live spectator events)
9. Anything purchased on eBay.
10. All of his old Led Zeppelin album covers.

Cuisine of Manland

Half the fun of traveling to a foreign country is taking in the local tastes of the region, and Manland has much to offer in this department. The joys that can spring from experiencing all the exciting flavors and delicacies of this culinary hot spot are endless. Rich in protein, carbs, and processed cheese, the Manland cuisine is one simply not to be missed by the most discerning of palates.

Local Delicacies

Despite one's temptation to fall back on the safety of the familiar menu of any one of the dozens of American fast-food chains that have cropped up around the world, the way to get the most bang for your tourist buck in Manland is to taste the lo-

The Five Food Groups of Manland

1. **Sugar:** Any glazed, frozen, or powdered food that is likely to send Man into a diabetic seizure and, thereby, kill him at a premature age.
2. **Salt:** Any tangy, tart, or spicy food that is likely to give Man high blood pressure and, thereby, kill him at a premature age.
3. **Cheese:** Any melted, orange, pasteurized food that is likely to knock Man's cholesterol into the triple digits and, thereby, kill him at a premature age.
4. **Meat:** Any section of an animal carcass that is likely to clog Man's arteries, and thereby, kill him at a premature age.
5. **Alcohol:** Any high-grain, chilled beverage that is likely to wipe out Man's liver functions and, thereby, kill him at a premature age.

cal delicacies. Just as a wise tourist wouldn't dream of visiting Paris without ordering a plate of escargot or . . . yikes! . . . little froggy legs, only a foolish Woman would journey all the way into the brush of Manland without feeding as the natives do. Below is your suggested Manland Dining Itinerary.

Breakfast

Breakfast occurs in Manland between the hours of 6:30 A.M. (if Man is employed) and 12 noon (if Man is unemployed) and is considered the artful culinary experience it is in that it is not so much *served*, as scrounged up. Whipped up on the spot much the way a brilliant French chef prepares a last-minute meal for a favored late-night arrival to his bistro, the process is simple, but artful in its execution.

Man begins seeking out his morning repast by inserting his head into the kitchen cabinets and pulling out a box of the finest dehydrated cuisine, imported from only the finest Manland factories of Kellogg's and General Mills. Then, much as Wolfgang Puck prepares a brunch for his celebrity guests in Hollywood, Man skillfully shakes the contents of the box into whatever roundish receptacle happens to be within reach, and soaks them for a carefully timed duration in a cool, white-colored liquid that has been chilling, like a fine wine, in the refrigerator.

National breakfast dish: Sugary cereal, such as Cocoa Pebbles, Fruity Pebbles, or Cap'n Crunch—left soaking in a bowl of milk for about a half hour, accompanied by four pounds of the finest Grade D bacon and a piece of lightly toasted bread. This banquet is usually finished off with a nice glass of cola served at room temperature.

Lunch

Lunch is consumed in Manland about an hour and a half after breakfast has been digested. It is hunted down by Man according to whichever food provider has the most accessible drive-thru window blinking the brightest neon sign. Lunchtime is a rushed time of day for Man—his mind is preoccupied not with his own needs, but with the ways in which he can help make the world a better place. So this meal must be not only nutritious and aesthetically pleasing, but also quick. Ever-obsessed with saving his money so he can donate it to charity, Man is a budget-conscious seeker of epicurean lunchtime delights, and focuses his efforts on midday specials such as: "Free pound of fries when you order ten pounds!"

National lunch dish: This meal consists of a delicious sandwich of some meat or other, topped with a healthy portion of exotically limp and brownish lettuce, a pale pink tomato, and a "special sauce," the recipe for which is kept under lock and key by the most influential chefs of the region. The meal is rounded out by French fries, a syrupy cola beverage in a container the size of a human head, and a "fresh baked" treat labeled "apple pie" that, miraculously, doesn't have any apples in it.

Special note: All Manland lunches are packaged in either Styrofoam or cellophane, and are presented neatly arranged on a tray or in a paper bag, allowing Man to transport his food easily from one location to another.

Dinner

Dinner in Manland is most often consumed during prime time television hours, and is a veritable feast for the body and soul.

Unlike Womanland, in which breakfast is the most important meal of the day, dinner is the priority in Manland. It incorporates all five of the major food groups and is the difference between life and death to Man. This is because several grueling hours exist in between Man's final meal of the day, and his breakfast of the next. Man must be able to live off his own body fat for the eight to ten hours he is sleeping. Dinner is the meal that enables him to do that.

National dinner dish: This evening feast begins with an exquisitely prepared appetizer of mozzarella cheese delicately breaded, then deep fried and served with a side selection of specially crafted dipping sauces such as ketchup, melted cheese, mayonnaise, and mustard—all presented in elegant Tupperware chafing dishes. This is followed by an entree consisting of a perfectly charred hunk of chopped meat, or meat byproduct, handcrafted into the shape of a large brick, drizzled with a Cheez Whiz topping. The entree is accompanied by a giant dish featuring an assortment of sides: mashed potatoes, beans, and, if it's a special occasion, broccoli sprinkled with melted Velveeta.

National dessert dish: Dessert is served immediately after dinner, and sometimes during it. It consists of anything fried, rolled, dipped, or drizzled in sugar.

Regional Manland Specialties

There are countless Manland recipes for which the greatest chefs of the world would kill. The common theme shared by each of these delights is that they are eaten by hand and cause massive heartburn. Here are just a few of the finest dishes you should seek out while on your trip:

1. *Beer nuts.*
2. *Nachos with beef, cheese, chili peppers, sour cream, and*

salsa. A favorite bar snack of Man, this delectable dish can be found in most neighborhood pubs.

3. *Hot dogs with chili, cheese, and onion.* Whether in the backyard or at the ballpark, Man enjoys this gooey delicacy during the warm summer months.

4. *Pizza.* Look for this doughy delight by the slice in neighborhood shops, or buy it in bulk from the local Costco (Man's store of choice) and enjoy it at home. Though it is best when served fresh out of the oven, Man often eats this dish cold, straight from the refrigerator, or at room temperature after it has sat out on the living room floor for a day or two.

5. *Buffalo wings.* Popular with the sports bar crowd in Manland, this ingenious dish combines the finger-lickin' hotness of Buffalo wings with the creamy coolness of ranch dressing. Try this snack while relaxing after a long day of sightseeing.

Beverages

As a general rule of thumb Man will suck down any beverage that contains either alcohol, caffeine, or sugar.

Another general rule of thumb: Man's favorite beverage is anything that is handed to him by someone with large breasts.

Eating Out (*Go ahead, laugh. It's funny.*)

When a tourist arrives in Japan, one of the greatest adjustments she has to make is learning how to eat Tokyo-style. She must remember to bow in between every course, master the mechanics of chopsticks, and get used to eating off of wood planks rather than plates. The same awareness of culinary etiquette will be called for when dining out in Manland. Some Manland customs will seem counterintuitive to you, but if you roll with them, you should come through with flying colors.

When dining out with Man:

1. Talk with your mouth full.
2. Shovel more food into your mouth before you are done chewing what is already in there.
3. Do not chew. Simply insert food directly into mouth, then swallow. If you choke, spit some of it back up into your mouth, then open your mouth and show off the chewed food in your mouth to your companion. Then reswallow.
4. Do not use the utensils provided by your server. Man has known for centuries that humans were born with their very own utensils attached right to their very person: thumb, pointer finger, and middle finger.
5. Avoid any food that is certified organic or anything found in nature. If you must eat something "natural," make sure you slather it in some sort of artificial sauce (Man prefers Cheez Whiz).
6. Burp in between every course.

Emergency Situations in Manland

Traveling to a foreign country can be a blast. But it can also be dangerous. You can lose your passport. Get tossed in a Mexican prison cell. Fall off the Eiffel Tower. Crushed by the Leaning Tower of Pisa. Gored while running with the bulls in Spain. Eaten by a tiger in South Africa. You get the idea.

Well, equally disastrous debacles can befall you while visiting Manland. At all times, you must be prepared for the plethora of destabilizing catastrophes that can occur when you venture into the heart and mind of the male species. Some of these calamities can be circumvented entirely by taking a few preemptive actions; the disrepair of others diminished considerably by performing a wee bit of damage control.

1. *The crisis:* Man has just dicovered that his recording of the best Super Bowl game ever has been recorded over with an episode of *Martha Stewart* entitled, "How to Clean Bathtub Tiles with Candle Wax." Man is hyperventilating himself into a state of unconsciousness, and threatening to take his own life . . . and yours before that.

   Damage control: Place Man in a reclining position on the couch, slap a moist cloth across his forehead, and hand him a bottle of tequila and the latest issue of *Playboy*. Assure him that he is mistaken, that his Super Bowl tape is simply in the other room. Then leave the house. For like, twelve hours. This gives Man enough time to get severely inebriated, and you enough time to go to a friend's house, hop online, and have a copy of that Super Bowl tape delivered overnight. Place the "missing" Super Bowl tape on Man's stomach the following morning before he awakes with a note attached reading, "Told you!" He'll feel so guilty for his false allegations that he'll buy you Godiva chocolates for at least a week!

2. *The crisis:* You are house-sitting for Man while he is on a business trip. The phone rings. You let the machine pick up. Man's ex-girlfriend, a Dutch model with breasts rumored to be so perky they could wave hello from across two continents speaks into the machine. *"Hi minnaar jongen, ben ik in stad yoor een zwempak tentoonstelling en wil u voor diner zien. Misschien iets meer? Roep mij."* This translates roughly to, "Hi lover boy, I am in town for a swimsuit exhibition, and want to see you for dinner. Maybe more? Call me." (You know this because you carry with you, at all times, a pocket English-Dutch dictionary for precisely these purposes.)

Damage control: Erase the message.

The Emotions of Man

While traveling through Manland, you may find yourself in any number of situations that call for you to interpret Man's emotions—much the way a pet owner must learn how to tell if little Fido is hungry or thirsty or needs to piddle. Because it is not in Man's nature to express feelings as a normal human being does, it is helpful to understand the cause-and-effect system that controls Man's emotions. This way, if you see the cause, you can anticipate the effect it will have on Man's emotional state. Nice and easy.

What Scares Man

Man has forever basked in the false image of being impervious to fear. Brave to a fault. Heroic and ballsy and all that jazz. But trust us, there is plenty that scares the bejesus out of Man.

1. Chick flicks
2. Dogs the size of small rodents
3. A female driver
4. Statues of naked Men
5. Tall Women
6. Lingerie with lots of clasps
7. Pregnancy tests
8. Organic food
9. PMS
10. Valentine's Day

What Makes Man Laugh

If you see that Man is in need of some cheering up, introduce any of the following to brighten his day. That frown of his will turn into a big, fat smile in no time. Because nothing makes Man laugh more than:

1. Watching a woman parallel park
2. Any movie with the Three Stooges in it
3. Anybody falling and hurting themselves
4. The sound of his own farts
5. The smell of his own farts
6. The sound of his own burps
7. The smell of his own burps
8. The sound or smell of your farts or burps

9. Your paycheck
10. Some of your hairdos

What Makes Man Cry

While seeing all the sights in Manland you may come across an inhabitant who is bawling like a baby. Here are the ten causes for his sadness. Do whatever you can to remove these crisis-inducing elements and Man will be immediately cured of his ills.

1. A broken television
2. A stripper with small breasts
3. A male secretary
4. An empty beer glass
5. An empty box of condoms
6. A visit from your mother
7. A dent in the fender
8. A plate of fresh vegetables
9. You saying, "Let's get married"
10. Some of your hairdos

What Makes Man Angry

It's no secret that Man has a temper. Heck. After that whole incident with the apple in the Garden of Eden, Adam didn't talk to Eve for like, days! So, it will come as no surprise that Man is capable of getting mad. Here are some of the things that can really tick off his testicles:

1. A speeding ticket
2. Poor satellite reception
3. A movie with no nude scenes

4. A dog that has to go out in the last ten seconds of the game
5. Being told to use a napkin
6. Inaccessible porn websites
7. Nagging
8. A candy wrapper that won't open
9. Another Man staring at your cleavage
10. A town with no car wash

What Makes Man Happy

The beauty of Man lies in his emotional simplicity. Ah, how easy it is to change his mood. No, it doesn't take much to make Man go from anger to jubilation. Any of these will do the trick:

1. Video games
2. You naked
3. Any female naked (except the fat neighbor—she makes Man cry)
4. Cheese
5. Beer
6. Cheese-flavored beer
7. Farting under the covers
8. Marathon episodes of *The A Team* in syndication
9. Getting out of a speeding ticket
10. Watching someone else *not* get out of a speeding ticket.

The Doctor Is In

Just as a doctor in Japan must battle language barriers when treating a sick patient from the U.S., you must learn how to cope with illness in Manland. You need to know how to translate Man's self-proclaimed symptoms into a rational diagnosis . . . and then treat him so he will quit his whining and stop giving you a headache.

Man whines: "Oh, my god, I'm dying."
Diagnosis: Man has a mild head cold.
Treatment: Hand Man a cup of chicken noodle soup and turn on the evening news so he can see footage of people dying horrible deaths in third world countries. That'll give Man perspective.

Man whines: "OH MY GOD! THE PAIN IS UNBEARABLE!"
Diagnosis: Man has stubbed his toe on the foot of the bed.
Treatment: Take out a package of frozen peas from the freezer and slap it on Man's "life threatening" injury. Then ignore Man for the rest of the night. The problem should be solved by morning.

Man whines: "I'll be in the bathroom."
Diagnosis: Man is constipated.
Treatment: Hand Man some car magazines, shove him into the bathroom with a few tablets of a stool softener, and speak to him in soothing tones. Promise him a club sandwich if he performs well.

Man whines: "Shhhhhhh!"
Diagnosis: Man is suffering from a hangover.
Treatment: First, smack Man upside the head because you warned him the night before not to chase beer with a shot of tequila. Then talk really loudly for the rest of the day.

Man whines: "Achoo! Achoo! Achoo!"
Diagnosis: Man is suffering from allergies to dust.
Treatment: Just say "Bless you" and go back to watching *The Office.*

Man whines: "I think they're going to have to amputate."
Diagnosis: Man has suffered a paper cut.
Treatment: Douse the cut with pure alcohol or any other type of burning liquid you have in your medicine chest, and place a bandage on the "wound."

Man whines: "Oohhhhhh (burp) God (fart)!"
Diagnosis: Severe and explosive diarrhea.
Treatment: Toss Man a bottle of Pepto Bismol, open all the windows, and get out of the house as fast as you can. Do not return for at least an hour.

Man whines: "I shouldn't have had that last nacho."
Diagnosis: Heartburn.
Treatment: Remove all the nachos from the house and replace them with fruit.

Man whines: "Why is it so hot in here?"
Diagnosis: Fever.
Treatment: Toss Man into a cold shower, then make him lie in bed and give him a rectal thermometer. (Not because you *need* to take his temperature, but just because it's funny!)

CHAPTER THREE

Manspeak: The Language of Manland

No man should travel until he has learned the language of the country he visits. Otherwise he voluntarily makes himself a great baby—so helpless and so ridiculous.

—Ralph Waldo Emerson

More difficult to translate than Swahili. More impossible to understand than Mandarin Chinese. Manspeak has confused Woman for centuries. Our inability to make sense of the muckety-muck that is Man's self-expression has launched opposing genders into myriad screaming matches in public, and been the cause of many an unnecessary breakup. Not to mention a violent homicide or two.

And while you can most certainly traverse the plains of Africa without knowing how to say "I am suffering from a severe case of explosive diarrhea" in Swahili, you absolutely, inarguably, and most certainly *cannot* venture into Manland without a clearer understanding of the mind-boggling language of its inhabitants. It is imperative that you learn how to interpret Man's coded language, everything from his pickup lines and dating declarations, to vocabulary and slang. Once you are able to tell which "I love you" means Man really loves you, and which means Man simply wants to have sex with you—*that* is the moment you have the power.

This chapter teaches you how to translate even the most complex of Manspeak phrases into something sensible and intelligent. In other words, Womanspeak.

Quick Pronunciation Guide

This pronunciation guide will provide you with helpful tricks for understanding the awkward language of Manland. While many of the sounds you'll hear in this ancient spoken dialect are common in languages throughout the world, there are certain pronunciations and usages unique to Manspeak that you'll need to get accustomed to in order to feel at home.

Sound	*Manland Usage*
Ā	"Y<u>a</u>y! *B<u>a</u>ywatch* is on in syndic<u>a</u>tion."
Ä	"Wanna smell my f<u>a</u>rt?"
A	"Hey, you pick up the t<u>a</u>b."
Aye	"<u>I</u> am wanting your sex."
Au	"I like my muffler l<u>ou</u>d."
B	"Can I touch your <u>b</u>utt?"
C	"<u>C</u>ocktail is a funny word, right?"
CH	"Wow, that's a long hair on your <u>ch</u>in."
D	"Are you, by chance, a 34 <u>DD</u>?"
E	"I lost my girlfriend in a b<u>e</u>t."
EE	"I have to fl<u>ee</u> the country."

F	"Mother F——ker!"
G	"That chili dog gave me gas."
H	"Please be my ho."
I	"Don't call me a twit."
J	"The doctor says it's jock itch."
Ji	"Gee, I dunno."
K	"Ick. I wish you had shaved."
L	"I love you . . . like a sister."
M	"I want my mommy."
N	"No doesn't really mean no, right?"
O	"I want my beer in a bottle."
OO	"Can I touch your boob?"
Oh	"Oh, I've got a boner."
Oi	"Fruit of my loins."
P	"I like to pee on white snow."
Ph	"Can I have your phone number?"
Q	"My Q-Tip is stuck in my ear."
R	"I have a rash on my genitals."
S	"Super Bowl Sunday"
Sh	"Shush! The game's on!"
T	"Touchdown!"
Th	"You've got a nice ath." (Man has a lisp.)
Th	"What the hell!"
U	"You've got a nice butt."
V	"Are you a virgin?"
W	"Wow, are those things real?!"
Wuh	"What's your name again?"
Y	"I'm horny."
Yun	"I'd like a deep fried onion."
Z	"Zzzzzzzzzzzzzzz."

English–Manspeak Dictionary

These are the words and phrases that comprise the fundamentals of conversation and social interaction in Manland. They will help you express yourself, as well as understand when the locals are attempting, in their own demented way, to express themselves to you. Practice these expressions until they become second nature.

Ambition: Getting off the couch.

Anniversary: That thing Man forgets about until he is inside the house.

Argument: To sit silently on the couch while Woman flaps her arms around in the air like a chicken, screaming and shouting her head off so loud the neighbors call the cops.

Attention Deficit Disorder: A pseudoclinical excuse for Man to not pay attention.

Be home soon: To come home sometime in the next forty-eight hours.

Be in love with: To be willing to buy tampons for.

Be on time: To be there within the hour.

Be romantic: To refrain from burping or farting.

Beating off: The act of pleasuring oneself. See also: peeling the banana, choking the chicken, playing the skin flute, burping the worm, punchin' the munchkin.

Birthday: For Man: the day on which Man gets a blowjob from Woman without reciprocation. For Woman: The day Man forgets to buy her a present.

Blue balls: A pseudoclinical excuse for Man to engage Woman in coitus.

On a break: Man is free to have sex with someone who is not his significant other.

Bro: Not, in fact, a relative, but an affectionate term Man uses for a pal with whom he drinks beer and discusses masturbation.

Can't: A word that is frequently employed by Man when he wishes to avoid a dreaded task or activity. For example, "I *can't* go to dinner at your mother's house this week" translates to "I *don't want to* go to dinner at your mother's house this week."

Cheating: Getting caught in a sexual act with someone other than girlfriend.

Chick flick: Any movie with Meg Ryan in it.

Clean: (Adjective) Anything that is not moldy, toxic, or emitting a rancid smell.

Clean: (verb) To wipe something down with dirty water.

Clean up: To make a killing at the racetrack.

Clean out: To empty junk from one thing and stick it in another thing.

Come clean: To admit to doing something bad only because Man got *caught* doing something bad.

Coitus interruptus: A phone call from Man's mother.

Commit: To let Woman leave a toothbrush in Man's bathroom.

Cuddle: An act of affection performed in the two to three seconds after sex, during which Man does nothing but fidget, sigh loudly, and check his watch.

Going out clubbin': An activity for which Man dresses in a ridiculous-looking suit, puts on too much cologne, and then pretends to be able to dance in order to look attractive to the female species.

Dog: A butt-ugly female.

Dawg: A cool dude.

Date (n.): An event during which Man attempts one-on-one social interaction with Woman in an effort to win her over. While Woman prefers dinner or a movie, Man's date of choice is sitting on the couch sharing the remote.

Diet: Short periods occuring several times a year in which Man puts less cheese on his food.

Dinner: Anything edible found in the fridge that isn't covered in mold.

Dining out: Man carrying his dinner plate from one end of the couch to the other.

Do-able: A woman with whom Man is willing to have sex.

Doing the laundry: Tossing all of one's clothing in the wash without separating by color or fabric, and praying for the best.

Doing the speed limit: To do the speed limit, plus 40 mph.

Drive safely: To operate a motor vehicle with fewer than three beers in one's system.

Dude: Slang for pal, friend, amigo, buddy, homeboy, bro.

Dump: 1. (noun) The act of releasing one's bowels, usually aided by the companionship of a car or motorcycle magazine. Example: "I have to take a dump." 2. (verb) To break off a romance with Woman. Example: "Yeah, I am gonna dump her."

Dying: To have the sniffles.

Eating out: The act of either performing oral sex on Woman, or calling for a pizza delivery. (Man enjoys both equally.)

Emote: To turn corners of one's mouth either upward or downward and hold steady for three seconds.

Ex: A female with whom Man had sex on more than one occasion who now hates his guts.

Exercise: Masturbation, lifting the remote, yawning.

Foreplay: Anything that delays Man's orgasm.

Get a beer: To suck down a six-pack.

Get dressed up: An action that occurs on or around a special occasion for which Man puts on a clean pair of underwear.

Get laid: To have sex.

Get laid off: To have sex while unemployed.

Gift: Something completely useless that Man buys Woman moments before realizing they are celebrating a special occasion.

Homo: Any fellow Man who dresses well, changes his sheets, and cleans his bathroom on a regular basis.

Horny: A state in which Man is overcome by the urge to stick his Manparts in a Woman's Ladyparts.

Huh?: The phrase commonly employed by Man when he is trying to determine the Who? What? When? Where? How? Why? of a given situation.

Jewelry: Anything shiny that can be hung around Woman's neck.

Kickoff: The moment the world must stop.

Lesbian: Any Woman who turns down Man's sexual overtures.

Listenin' to some tunes: Blasting the car stereo so loud it trembles the walls of the houses in neighboring counties.

Major hottie: A very sexy female.

M.I.L.F.: An attractive mother, usually considerably older, with whom Man desires to fornicate.

No: Stock answer employed whenever Woman asks Man if he did something wrong.

Old: Any female over the age of twenty-two.

Porn: Anything that can be masturbated to.

Power: To hold the remote in one's hand.

Cell Phone Manspeak

Man employs a whole different language when communicating via a cell phone. Here's the 411 on what you can expect from a casual phone conversation with Man while he is roaming the plains of his natural habitat.

Man says: "Yo."
Translation: "Greetings, fellow citizen."

Man says: "What's up?"
Translation: "How are you this fine day?"

Man says: "Yep!"
Translation: "Yes, I quite agree with your statement."

Man *says:* "Huh?"
Translation: "I'm so sorry, but there seems to be some static on the line. Would you mind repeating your last statement for me?"

Man says: "Nah."
Translation: "I'm so sorry, truly, but that just is not possible at this juncture in time."

Man says: "Sure."
Translation: "Why, of course! It would be my pleasure."

Man says: "No way!"
Translation: "I simply cannot believe what you are telling me—it shocks me to the core."

Man says: "See ya!"
Translation: "Although this is a mere colloquialism, I do
    hope that we bump into each other in the near
    future—or at least speak again soon on the phone as
    this has been such a pleasure."

Man says: "Later."
Translation: "I hope we can continue
    this discussion at another time."

Quiche: Something Man does not eat.

Reading: Leafing through a porno magazine or skimming the
    back of a cereal box.

Religious experience: An orgasm.

Remember: To forget until the very last minute.

Return a phone call: To get around to calling back the person
    who left the message about six days ago.

Run an errand: Something that Man always forgets to do.

Safe sex: Any sexual act that doesn't result in a groin muscle
    injury.

Sensitive: Wimpy.

Score: To get laid . . . or to make a goal or touchdown during
    a sporting event.

Spending quality time together: Sitting on the same side of the
    couch . . . maybe naked.

Swamp Ass: A collection of condensation that gathers in the
male buttocks region due to extreme perspiration. Often
causes itchiness, rash, and incessant whining.

Take a nap: What Man says he is going to do when is he
planning to sleep for the next twelve to fourteen hours,
usually on the sofa where you are trying to read.

Take a shower: Splashing cologne under one's armpits.

Thanksgiving dinner: A meal that interferes with the
television broadcast of the Dallas Cowboys kickoff.

Think hard: To furrow one's brow, chew on one's bottom lip,
and blink intermittently.

Underwear: A nonessential item of clothing.

Valentine's Day: Most annoying day of the year.

Watching the game: To spend four hours yelling at the
television in a desperate attempt to get the referee to listen.

Working out: Daily or weekly activity in which Man stands
in front of the mirror at the gym, admiring his muscles and
flexing whenever a female in a leotard strolls by.

XXX: The best movies ever.

ZZZZZZ: Man is asleep. Don't wake him.

Useful Commands

When visiting a busy metropolis like New York City, tourists
quickly learn that the squeaky wheel gets the oil, so to speak.
If a visitor fails to shout at the top of her lungs to the subway
conductor, "Hold the train!" she will get crushed in the doors
and dragged to her death. Manland is no different.

In order to get what you want, and avoid getting what you
don't want, you must assert yourself loudly and clearly. No
mincing of words. By nature, Man is a defiant creature. He

thinks in simple terms and doesn't get subtlety. You have to take the guesswork out of your commands for Man—tell him precisely what you want and don't sugar coat it. Unless you are completely direct, Man will find ways to squirm out of the simplest of instructions. So, if you want something done, or not done, shout one of these commands at him. And smack him with a newspaper for added effect.

"No means no!"

"Get away from me, you pervert!"

"Don't talk with your mouth full!"

"Buying me dinner doesn't mean you get sex!"

"Stop snoring! You're shaking the walls!"

"Clean up this mess!"

"Not tonight! I told you I have a headache."

"Put the toilet seat down!"

"My God, close the friggin' door when you use the bathroom!"

"Send your mother a birthday card, dammit, or I'll slit your throat while you sleep!"

"No, you cannot touch my breast!"

"Wash your hands!"

"Turn the television down!"

Overheard in Manland

Just as Eve threw Adam into a tizzy when she shook things up in the Garden of Eden, the locals of Manland can get slightly freaked out by visiting female tourists. They often deem Woman's pragmatism, intelligence, and exemplary personal hygiene habits as a threat to their society, and they may lash out verbally if they fear their space is being invaded or their lifestyle is in danger of being altered. Should this occur, and you are attacked with any of the following verbalizations, simply maintain steady eye contact, allow Man to express himself, and then

ignore him . . .

"Hand me my beer."
"I *did* put the toilet seat down."
"Let the machine get it."
"Quit nagging me."
"Huh?"
"I dunno."
"Can we have sex?"
"I wasn't touching myself!"
"I showered yesterday."
"It just *looked* like I was pinching her ass!"
"How come you didn't remind me?"
"These clothes are clean."

Things You Must Never Say in Manland

Just as you shouldn't order a wiener schnitzel in Israel, there are certain key phrases you should never utter when cavorting in Manland. Man does not like being publicly reprimanded, interrogated, served ultimatums, instructed to perform tasks he deems "feminine," or forced to express his emotions. So, in order to ensure your safety while touring this magnificent countryside, it's best to avoid murmuring the following phrases to any of Manland's citizens.

"Who do you think you are?"
"Your friend is cute."
"You'd never cheat on me, right?"
" . . . or *else!*"
"I want to talk about my feelings."
"This time, I'm really serious."
"Wake up! I said wake up!"
"Football is soooo boring."
"You should call your mother."
"How many beers have you had?"
"Do you think she's pretty?"
"Do I look fat?"
"Am I the best sex you've ever had?"
"Is it always that small?"
"You call *that* a thoughtful gift?"
"I just want to be friends."
"Maybe you should try that Rogaine stuff?"
"I told my mother she could come live with us."
"I need you to cancel boys night out."
"Your team sucks."
"Maybe you're just nervous . . ."
"It's either your friends, or me. You choose."

CHAPTER FOUR

Shopping in Manland

Give a girl a shopping mall and all is right
with the world!

—Tammy Faye Bakker

Travelers flock to Switzerland to bring home the finest chocolates. They blast off to Ireland to stock up on the finest whiskey. Well, your trip to Manland should have you returning to terra firma no less weighed down with glorious goods. Bringing home souvenirs from this magical land enables you to instantly transport yourself back to the wonderment that was your vacation to Manland anytime you wish. Classic issues of *Playboy*. Bronzed footballs. Fuzzy dice for your car's rearview mirror. Each holds a fond memory that will live in your mind and heart forever.

And the best souvenir of all . . . the one that most tourists fly to Manland in search of . . . the Holy Grail of the male kingdom? It's finding *the* Man of your dreams.

But shopping for your Manland souvenir can be a daunting experience. There are so many specialty stores to explore, so many versions of Man to choose from. So, before you can decide which keepsake is the best investment, you need to know the varieties of Man available, and how they can each serve your personal needs.

The information provided below will help you determine which product is worth claiming at Customs.

Clothing Makes the Man . . . but What Does It Make Him, Exactly?

They say clothing makes the Man. Ah, but makes him *what*? That, dear girl, is the question. Don't rush into getting the perfect Manland souvenir! Do some window shopping before you commit. You can tell a lot about Man by the duds he sports. Knowing the basics of the Manland Dress Code will help you size up Man from a safe distance, leaving you free to either pursue a potentially good bargain, or flee to another flea market.

The Manland Dress Code

When you're souvenir shopping it is often the packaging that first grabs your eye. The external appearance of a product can tell you a lot about what is inside, making it easy to see which Manland souvenirs are worth picking off the shelf for closer examination. Take note of Man's wardrobe. Particular items of clothing signify particular personality traits.

Standard White Shirt, Blue Tie, and Pleated Slacks

This Man is successful in business and has a job that provides great medical benefits, a promising stock portfolio, and access to powerful computer software. You may enjoy his ability to provide you with the creature comforts, but be forewarned: He is married to his job and his preferred form of communication is sending you egregiously typo-filled messages from his BlackBerry.

Tattered Jeans and a Metallica Shirt

This Man has dedicated his life to preserving the halcyon days of 1980s heavy metal. He is a fun-loving nostalgic who lives life to the fullest and does not leave the house without hairspray. He sports a "f—you" attitude to anything he perceives as "the establishment." He is also half deaf and likely to make you listen to him play "Enter Sandman" on his guitar day in and day out.

Levi's Jeans, Cowboy Shirt, Cowboy Boots, and a Cowboy Hat

This Man is a hardworking cowboy with a chiseled body and unwavering respect for the land of his forefathers. He can get you free grade A beef anytime you want. Unfortunately, he sometimes gets lonely on the prairie at night and slips some of his own grade A beef to the sheep.

Black Pants, Black Coat, Black Pilgrim Hat

This Man is Amish, and thereby sweet, honest, God-fearing, and can churn his own butter. Downside is it's gonna take him about four hours to pick you up for dates, as he drives a horse and buggy.

Black Turtleneck, Black Leather Pants, Dark Sunglasses

This Man is a staunch observer of the beatnick culture, which had its heyday in the 1960s. He is an intense and thought-provoking artist who paints in his studio in the late hours of the night and reads Kafka and Tolstoy for fun. He will encourage you to think and challenge authority . . . but may bore you to death in the process.

Plaid Pants, Button-Down Three-Quarter-Sleeve Shirt, Thick Black Glasses, Pocket Protector, Pants Hiked Up Above the Navel

This Man is a geek. He can fix any computer problem you have, recite the entire Encyclopedia Britannica verbatim, and is fluent in Vulcan. But as a general rule, this Man does not have much experience dealing with the female gender. Teaching him how to please a Woman, both socially and physically, could take years. Or, as he would tell you in Vulcan, "tevuns."

Fake Gucci Suit and Fake Prada Loafers

This Man works in the "waste management" profession, and pays for everything with cash. He has a nickname like "Eddie The Machete" and seems to constantly be attending funerals. Dating him will get you the best tables at the best Italian restaurants. But don't think long-term with this guy . . . as he probably won't be alive too much longer.

Bermuda Shorts, Hawaiian Shirt, Flip-flops, Rayban Sunglasses

This Man is a highly immature, laid-back surfer dude who considers waking up by noon "being responsible." He doesn't have a job, per se, but makes money on the side by dealing in hashish, and is a bit of a player with the ladies. He tends to be of a spiritual nature and will introduce you to the basics of Buddhism to help you find inner peace. But it's worth noting that this Man is probably helping a *lot* of women find their inner peace.

Impeccable Designer Tuxedo (on Loan)

This Man is a Hollywood star with a multi-million-dollar income. He plays poker with the likes of Matt Damon and George Clooney, and brings home great "swag" from all the awards shows he attends. He can fly you to Rome for dinner on his private jet, pamper you in his mansion up in the Hollywood Hills, and introduce you to all his famous friends. But there is a downside to all of this glamour. You'll never know if that's his real nose.

Army Fatigues and Combat Boots

This Man is a military dude, which means he is disciplined, patriotic, chivalric, reliable, punctual, physically fit, brave, and willing to die for his country. He is a stand-up guy who believes in honoring tradition, which means you will never have to open another door for yourself or worry about this guy forgetting your birthday. He will make you feel like a lady every single day because he's an officer and a gentleman. Unfortunately, though, this Man also blends in with the foliage, which makes finding him for dinner really tough.

Greenpeace T-shirt, Shorts Made of Recycled Toilet Tissue, and Birkenstocks

This Man is a peace-loving environmentalist who wants to make the world a better place. In other words, he volunteers for organizations that help the less fortunate. Unfortunately, for you, that means he will think nothing of dragging you to a third world country to build irrigation ditches and live in a hut with tribespeople who have giant elephant tusks rammed through their nostrils.

Mesh Sports Jersey, Mesh Sports Shorts, Mesh Baseball Cap—All with Matching Team Logo

This Man is a fun-loving, beer-guzzling, home-team-rootin' guy who devotes his life to cheering on his favorite teams. He can rattle off every sports statistic in history, but the only letters of the alphabet he knows are ESPN. He's the souvenir you want around when you're in the mood to have a good time— his inherent joie de vivre is contagious. But God help you if you want him to have a deep conversation . . . the only "deep" this Man knows is "deep dish pizza."

Technicolor Silk Cape, Skin-Tight Velvet Purple Pants, Heeled Boots, Floppy Hat

This Man is a pimp. He always has plenty of cash on him and is quite popular with all the other Men in the neighborhood. He has a massive entourage of security personnel to keep you safe and sound at all times, and transports you in style in his brand new, fully loaded Cadillac Escalade. The downside? This Man takes a 50 percent cut of your annual salary and calls you his "ho."

Orange Vest, Orange Hat, Khaki Pants with Lots of Pockets, Gun Case

This Man is an avid hunter who has precision aim, can imitate all sorts of animal mating calls, and is able to provide food for you at all times (provided there are woods around and he remembered to apply for his hunter's permit). He is respectful of nature, and believes in the simple things. Oh, and he's really easy to spot in a crowd . . . especially at a PETA rally.

Fedora, Black Slacks, Black Trenchcoat

This Man is a secret agent for the CIA which means he will bring gifts from exotic places and can translate foreign films for you. The downside is he is never around, and you'll probably never know his real name.

Flannel Shirt, Torn Jeans, Nirvana T-shirt

This Man is a devotee of the Seattle rock scene of the early to mid 1990s. He's laid back, and has no needs outside of his cup of java and an acoustic guitar. He will teach you to take the road less traveled and avoid conforming to the status quo. He will also teach you that showering only once a week helps protect the nation from a drought.

**Pants Hanging Below the Waistline, 120 Pounds
of Gold Bling-bling Draped Around the Neck,
Shaquille O'Neal Basketball Jersey,
Spankin' New Nike High-tops**

This Man is a wannabe gangsta rapper. He can break dance with the best of them and knows every word to every Eminem and 50 Cent song. He will drape you in bling the size of car hood ornaments and get you into the best nightclubs in the city. But because he carries a veritable arsenal of weapons at all times, getting through airport security with this Man is, as he would say, a "bitch."

Internet Shopping in Manland

Nowadays, thanks to the wonders of the Internet (a big thanks to you, Al Gore!), a tourist can also shop for her Manland souvenir from the safety of her hotel room. Millions of Manland citizens use the Internet to advertise their marketability to tourists. Internet souvenir shopping is wonderfully convenient, and you can have a great deal of fun browsing the market. But window shopping in Manland cyberspace can also be dangerous. Man likes to take advantage of the anonymity the online selling market provides to exaggerate the truth, or, in some cases, fabricate it entirely. It's up to you to read between the key strokes and figure out what he's *really* saying.

For example, if Man's Internet profile describes him as "successful," that could mean he's *successful*-ly living the life of a complete loser. Nor does it matter if Man claims to be "cute." A wombat can be "cute." And if he claims he's a "nice guy"? Forget it. Ted Bundy was a "nice guy"—until he killed about three hundred women.

Clues to Man's genuine character are hidden in every self-promoting declaration he makes in cyberspace. Learn to spot them, or you'll end up returning from your vacation with a wombat. Or worse yet, another Ted Bundy.

Man claims: "My name is John."
Translation: "My name is Hubert, but I don't like to admit it."

Man claims: "I look for honesty, intelligence, and wit in a Woman."
Translation: "I look for big boobs, a tight butt, and rich parents in a Woman."

Man claims: "My idea of a romantic date is holding hands as we stroll along the beach, and then volunteering together at the local soup kitchen."
Translation: "My idea of a romantic date is watching three pornos in a row and then acting them out in front of a video camera."

Man claims: "The last book I read was *War and Peace*."
Translation: "The last book I read was the Cliff Notes for *War and Peace*."

Man claims: "I'm religious about going to the gym."
Translation: "I'm religious about thinking about going to the gym."

Man claims: "I'm a concert pianist."
Translation: "I own one of those electronic keyboard things and can play *Chopsticks*."

Man claims: "My favorite movies are *Die Hard, Die Hard 2: Die Harder, Die Hard with a Vengeance*, and *Live Free or Die Hard*."
Translation: "I'm straight."

Man claims: "My favorite movies are *Gone With the Wind, Meet Me in St. Louis*, and *The Sound of Music*."
Translation: "I'm gay."

Man claims: "My ideal Woman is smart, passionate, and loves animals."
Translation: "My ideal Woman is smarter than a fruit fly, but dumber than me, horny as a toad, and willing to do things on camera with animals."

Man claims: "I am a staunch environmentalist."
Translation: "I occasionally recycle my beer cans."

Man claims: "I'm successful."
Translation: "I'm successful at flipping burgers at McDonald's."

Man claims: "I love kids."
Translation: "I love kids because they make me look more mature."

Man claims: "I'm looking to settle down and grow old with someone special."
Translation: "I may get terminally ill and want someone around to change my bedpan when things take a turn for the worse."

Man claims: "I'm sensitive."
Translation: "I know how to fake cry."

Man claims: "I'm a Republican."
Translation: "I'm rich."

Man claims: "I'm a Democrat."
Translation: "I'm poor."

Man claims: "I'm a liberal Republican."
Translation: "I'm rich . . . and secretly gay."

Man claims: "Jesus is my guide."
Translation: "Satan is my guide, but that doesn't go over too
    well with Women."

Man claims: "I like foreign films."
Translation: "I like foreign films because they show nipples."

Man claims: "I'm a doctor."
Translation: "I watch *ER*."

Man claims: "I'm recently single."
Translation: "I haven't been laid in so long my genitals are
    growing cobwebs."

Man claims: "This is the first time I've tried online dating."
Translation: "I've been doing this crap since 1998."

Man claims: "I'm a bit of a loner."
Translation: "I'm a serial killer."

Man claims: "I like Women who are into sports."
Translation: "I don't like fat Women."

Man claims: "I like a Woman who does yoga."
Translation: "I like a Woman who can hold her ankles behind her ears."

Man claims: "I prefer a casual dining experience."
Translation: "I'm cheap."

Man claims: "I'm in great shape."
Translation: "I have all my appendages."

Man claims: "I volunteer for several charities."
Translation: "I tossed a buck in the donation slot at a church one time."

Man claims: "I'm tall, dark, and handsome."
Translation: "I'm short, albino, and freakish looking."

Man claims: "I'm looking to settle down."
Translation: "My mother is kicking me out of the house."

Man claims: "I own a boat."
Translation: "I have an inflatable raft left over from my Boy Scout days."

Man claims: "Yeah, I've got some really major business deals on the horizon."
Translation: "I'm selling all my used DVDs on eBay."

Man claims: "I didn't have any interest in going to college."
Translation: "I didn't get into any colleges."

Man claims: "I've been traveling a lot lately."
Translation: "I just escaped from prison."

Man claims: "People tell me I look like a cross between Brad Pitt and Johnny Depp."
Translation: "I have hair and eyes."

Man claims: "I have a degree in English literature."
Translation: "I have a degree in bullshit."

Man claims: "I have an open mind."
Translation: "I'll have sex with pretty much anyone and anything."

Man claims: "I'm close with my mother."
Translation: "I live with my mother."

Man claims: "I'm in between jobs right now."
Translation: "I'm unemployed."

Common Pickup Lines

If shopping for your Manland souvenir online isn't your cup of tea, tourists who prefer interaction with the locals often find a variety of products from which to choose in the Manland bar scene.

This is where male citizens of all shapes and sizes come to drink and make flagrant, and often pathetic, attempts to get laid. And for all the suffering a female tourist will experience at the hands of such aggression, a Woman in a Manland bar may as well slather herself in chum and dive into shark-infested waters. If you find yourself in a Manland bar, inevitably you will be the target of every jackass in the room looking for a little validation. In an attempt to get "some action," Man will slither up to you as you sit perched on your barstool and strike up a conversation. He will use every line in the book to lower your defenses and charm the cargo pants off you. But do not be fooled. When properly decoded, Bar Man speak reveals the true intentions fueling this cunning creature's every move. The sooner you know how to read between the lines, the easier it will be to weed out the putzes from the princes.

Man says: "Hi."
Translation: "I want to have sex."

Man says: "How are you?"
Translation: "I still want to have sex with you."

Man says: "Pardon me, is this seat taken?"
Translation: "I plan on hovering over you no matter what your answer is."

Man says: "Can I buy you a drink?"
Translation: "The less sober you are, the easier this will be for me."

Man says: "Come here often?"
Translation: "Are you an alcoholic?"

Man says: "Do you live around here?"
Translation: "Sex on a bed would be so much easier than in that bathroom stall over there, yes?"

Man says: "Are you here alone?"
Translation: "If I were to kidnap you and chain you to a pipe in my basement, would anyone notice you were gone?"

Man says: "You look like you're into yoga."
Translation: "You look like you can bend in five hundred different ways."

Man says: "I'm not into the bar scene."
Translation: "I'm here pretty much every night and losing hope fast."

Man says: "You have beautiful eyes."
Translation: "You have beautiful breasts."

Man says: "I'm a really nice guy."
Translation: "My ex-girlfriends all think I'm a sleaze bag."

Man says: "Let's step outside a minute."
Translation: "I just spotted my ex-girlfriend across the room."

Man says: "You can trust me."
Translation: "You can't trust me."

Man says: "I just broke up with someone."
Translation: "I just got dumped."

Man says: "I've never felt such a connection so instantly with anyone."
Translation: "I tried this line on a girl the other night and she actually went home with me."

Man says: "I'm not like other guys."
Translation: "The only thing that distinguishes me from every other doofus in this bar is my Social Security number."

Man says: "I could just sit and talk to you for hours."
Translation: "I could just sit and talk to you about myself for hours."

Man says: "I'd love to get to know you better."
Translation: "I'd love to get you naked and then cover you in whipped cream."

Man says: "You have a very exotic look about you."
Translation: "Are you an illegal immigrant?"

Man says: "Are you a natural blonde?"
Translation: "Can you add two plus two without the assistance of a calculator?"

Man says: "My apartment is being exterminated."
Translation: "My girlfriend is home."

Helpful Responses to Cheesy Pickup Lines

Knowing how to spot a pathetic come-on in a Manland pickup joint is a powerful tool you will use over and over again on your trip. But identifying the disease is only half the battle, missy. Curing it is the key. When you find yourself the victim of unwanted advances from Man, make use of any of these handy responses to extricate yourself with immediacy and ease. This will free you up to continue shopping for a worthwhile souvenir in peace and quiet.

Jerk says: "Pardon me, but is this seat taken?"
You respond: "No. And let's keep it that way."

Jerk says: "Haven't I seen you in some magazine?"
You respond: "Yes, you have. But you really shouldn't admit to reading gay porn."

Jerk says: "I'll have whatever she's having."
You respond: "I'm having a baby. Thanks for offering to help."

Jerk says: "What's your sign?"
You respond: (Hold up your middle finger.)

Jerk says: "You're a model, right?"
You respond: "And you're an idiot, right?"

Jerk says: "You have beautiful eyes."
You respond: "All the better to see that you don't stand a chance in hell."

Jerk says: "I really want to get to know you."
You respond: "It's good to want things."

Jerk says: "What? This silly thing? Nah, it's not a wedding ring."
You respond: "Funny, that's the same thing your wife said to that guy over there."

Jerk says: "I don't usually do this kind of thing."
You respond: "Good, because you suck at it."

Jerk says: "What do you say we blow this popsicle stand and go back to my place?"
You respond: "What do you say you just go back to your place and blow yourself?"

Jerk says: "I feel such a connection with you."
You respond: "Good. Then try feeling it long distance."

Jerk says: "Is it me, or were we meant to be together?"
You respond: "It's you."

Jerk says: "I'm not like other guys . . ."
You respond: "You mean you're like other women?"

Jerk says: "I've got a hot tub back at my place."
You respond: "Good, go drown yourself in it."

Jerk says: "What's a woman like you doing in a place like this?"
You respond: "Trying to avoid jackasses like you."

Jerk says: "I think we've met somewhere before."
You respond: "I think so, too. And you failed miserably that time as well."

The Art of Seduction in Manland

Man is a sexual creature by nature. Almost anything arouses him. So, while a Woman's natural instinct is to go through the hell of waxing every hair follicle on her body and squeezing into some ridiculously complicated Victoria's Secret lingerie contraption, seduction in Manland doesn't call for such extreme preparation. Man can be turned on faster than a light switch by much simpler means. Try any of these:

1. Balance a plate of deep-fried pork on your bare breasts.
2. Call Man on his cell phone and recite the batting averages of his favorite baseball players.
3. Ask to watch Man clip his toenails over the bathroom sink.
4. Let Man watch you clip your toenails over the bathroom sink.
5. Shampoo your hair with beer.
6. Tattoo Man's favorite football team's logo on your buttocks.
7. Screen your mother's calls.
8. Don't wash away that layer of thick mold growing on the shower curtain.
9. Light candles all over the house and then play a recording of baby seals being slaughtered in the Arctic.
10. Tell Man he can go watch the game with his buddies.

Common First Date Activities

So, let's say your Manland shopping excursion has been a success. After searching high and low though the country's vast market of goods for the perfect souvenir, you have finally found one you think might be worth investing in. But just as you wouldn't dream of laying down a hundred bucks for a wool sweater in a Scottish souvenir shop before trying it on, it is best to spend some quality time with this potential Man companion before you actually purchase him. Take him out for a test drive, to make certain that he passes all the Customs rules and such.

You can tell a lot about what kind of souvenir Man will make by the Manland destination he chooses for your first date. Beneath his choice of venue lies a great deal of Man subtext.

Location	*What It Means*
The zoo	"I didn't shower this morning and hope the monkeys will upstage my own stink."
The beach	"I'd really like to see what you look like in a bathing suit . . . plus, my feet need some serious exfoliation and sand is great for that."
On a motor-cycle ride	"I like the freedom of the open road and enjoy the thrill of not knowing whether my date will fall off the back or not."
Scuba diving	"I like the 'wet' look."
The museum	"I want you to think me an intellectual, but the truth of the matter is I just like seeing the statues of naked women in the Greek sculpture section."

The local car show	"I totally forgot about the car show when I asked you out and didn't know how to get out of this."
Hiking in the mountains	"I love nature, and how easy it'll be to lose you if we end up not hitting it off."
Bowling	"I'm determined to stick my fingers in *something* tonight . . . even if it's a big ball."
An amuse-ment park	"Vomit turns me on, and I'm willing to shell out $1,000 to win a $3 stuffed animal."
A walk in the park	"I'm really cheap, and the dog needs a walk anyway, so I'm killing two birds with one stone."
A rock concert	"I'm not really sure what to say to you for two hours, so this should keep things simple. Plus, I like to get stoned."
A picnic	"I want you to think I'm romantic even though we both know there is nothing romantic about sitting on the grass with ants crawling all over us, eating food that's been sitting in a basket for two hours under the blazing sun."
Dinner at his parents' house	"My folks think I'm gay, and this will throw them off the track."
Arena sporting event	"My buddy bailed on me at the last minute, so it's a good thing you were free to fill in the empty seat."
Broadway musical	"I'm either gay, or considering turning gay."
The ballet	"I am comfortable enough with my mascu-linity to spend a few hours staring at men with large bulges in their tights."

The opera	"I am an insomniac and take the phrase 'sleeping with a girl' literally."
Apple picking	"I secretly despise Women and blame your gender for the fall of Man."
Horseback riding	"Nothing makes me feel closer to a Woman than following her on a trail of manure."
Starbucks	"I have never had an original thought in my head."
A bar with his friends	"I don't trust my own judgment, so I've got all my boys checking you out as well."
The movies	"If we don't make out during the film, at least I got some popcorn out of the deal."
Professional wrestling match	"I'm pretty sure I'm straight, and yet, I find myself strangely drawn to oversized men dressed in leotards."
On his private jet to Italy for dinner	"You are soooo lucky I am bothering with you."
A nightclub	"If things don't work out with you, maybe I can go home with someone sluttier."
Ice skating	"I'm romantic, traditional, and really like Celine Dion songs."
A rodeo	"At least I'll see humping in some form tonight."
A horror film	"I'm hoping you'll be so scared you'll leap into my arms and inadvertently brush against my genital region."
A foreign-film marathon	"I want you to fall asleep with your head in my lap."

| A postage-stamp expo | "I am the most boring Man on Earth." |
| An action movie | "I am determined to see this movie with or without you—you are a mere accessory." |

Movie Theater Body Language

You can tell a lot about Man's intentions on your date by his body language. If he . . .

1. Seats you both in the back of the theater: Man plans on making a pass at you once the movie starts.
2. Buys a chili dog at the concession stand: Man has no intention of making a pass at you.
3. Gets up repeatedly: Man ate too much popcorn and now has diarrhea.
4. Stretches and yawns dramatically, then rests his arm on the back of your chair: Man is trying to cop a feel (oldest trick in the book, but the idiots still do it).
5. Fidgets and sighs intermittently: Man is bored by either you or the movie.

First-Date Restaurants

When you book a trip with a travel agent, one of the first things he/she explains is that the location of your hotel is key. It's the factor that can make or break your holiday stay. Well, the same rule applies for restaurant destinations in Manland.

Once Man has either charmed or horrified you with his choice of first-date venue, he will inevitably suggest that you go out to "grab somethin'" to eat. (Much like the great white shark, Man cannot function for more than a few hours without shoving something into his mouth.) That being said, you can tell a lot about Man not only by the food he eats, but from the places at which he dines.

Location	*Translation*
A roadside hot dog truck	"I am a cheap bastard with a future of of gastrointestinal problems to look forward to."
A roadside hot dog truck with picnic tables	"I'm a cheap bastard with a future of gastrointestinal problems, but I still want to take the time to get to know you."
A roadside truck that sells hot dogs and fried seafood	"I'm a cheap bastard, and willing to expose you to *E. coli*, but am also thoughtful enough to offer you a choice between low-grade beef and low-grade shellfish."
A roadside truck that only sells veggie burgers	"I'll do anything to protect the rights of animals, but couldn't care less about killing innocent chunks of tofu."
A fast-food joint	"I want to keep this date short."

The drive-thru window of a fast-food joint	"I want to keep this date *really* short."
A sushi restaurant	"I am extravagant, worldly, culturally aware, but have no idea how to use a fork."
An Ethiopian restaurant	"I am aware of the social plight in third world countries, and even more aware of the irony of there being a restaurant like this."
A hole-in-the-wall Italian restaurant on a side street in Little Italy	"I am connected to the Mob, and it is likely that someone will whack me while you suck the cream out of my cannoli."
An Olive Garden	"I'm not connected to the Mob in any way but want you to think I am. . . . Plus we get unlimited salad and breadsticks."
A four-star restaurant where he lets you order only off the prix fixe menu	"I want to impress you, but only with a choice between three appetizers and three entrees, and dessert with coffee or tea—no substitutions."
A four-star restaurant where he lets you order à la carte	"I want to impress you . . . just please don't order the lobster because that's market price."

A picnic in the park	"I want to be in a very public place in case you turn out to be a psycho."
Ramen noodles at his place	"I have no money, but think highly enough of you to go through the hassle of boiling water."
Ordering in at his place	"I like making delivery guys pedal around on their bikes in the rain."
Cooks a gourmet meal for you at his place	"I am a skilled chef, and eating at my place makes it so much easier to get you into the bedroom."

First-Date Manspeak

The difference between that beautiful necklace you brought home from your vacation to Mexico last year, and the beautiful Man you are going to bring home from this trip is that the latter talks. And therein lies the problem. There you are at the restaurant, your body squeezed, sausagelike, into a dress two sizes too small, wobbling around in heels so high you need crutches to move two feet in any direction. You barely understand the menu and have no idea what time zone you are in. To top it off, rather than being able to just sit back and enjoy the view, you have to listen carefully to what Man says while on this first date. What comes out of his mouth can help you decide whether this souvenir is a keeper or not.

For instance, when Man says he finds you "interesting," is he saying that because he truly does? Or does he find the thought of you downing six martinis and ending up naked in his bed interesting? Is Man, in fact, the affluent bank president he claims to be? Or does he work part time as a serial killer, and have plans to chop you up into tiny bits with a pocket knife, then stash your dismembered body parts in his refrigerator? And perhaps, most important, when Man tells you to order "anything you like" off the menu, does he really mean "anything"?

The sooner you know what you're dealing with, the sooner you can decide whether this is a model of Man you are interested in bringing back to the mainland with you. (And if you're allowed to order the lobster.)

Travel Tips: *Man's Appearance*

Give Man constant praise whenever he is looking particularly fit, well-dressed, and well-groomed. If you fail to do so, Man will think nothing of not showering for days and recycling his underwear.

Man says: "Sorry I'm late."
Translation: "I was hiding behind some bushes outside so I could make sure you weren't a complete dog."

Man says: "My car broke down, so I had to take a cab."
Translation: "I don't own a car—I took the bus."

Man says: "Allow me to pull out your chair."
Translation: "Let me take a peek at your ass."

Man says: "Shellfish causes gout."
Translation: "Don't you dare order the lobster."

Man says: "Huh. Funny. There are no prices on the menu."
Translation: "Oh crap, this is a four-star restaurant!"

Man says: "I like your sweater."
Translation: "I like how your boobs look in that
   sweater."

Man says: "Order anything you like off the menu."
Translation: "For every dollar you cost me, I get to touch
   your breast one time."

Man says: "So, tell me about yourself."
Translation: "Tell me about yourself, but I won't listen to a
   word you say."

Man says: "My last girlfriend was too clingy."
Translation: "I cheated on my last girlfriend."

Man says: "When's your birthday?"
Translation: "How old are you?"

Man says: "Excuse me. I have to use the men's room."
Translation: "Excuse me, I have to go jerk off."

Man says: "Oh, my hair's so short because I'm in the
   military."
Translation: "I'm going bald."

Man says: "I'm all for equal rights for Women."
Translation: "You're picking up the check, right?"

Man says: "How many boyfriends have you had?"
Translation: "Are you a slut?"

Man says: "I don't speak to any of my exes."
Translation: "I chopped up all my exes into tiny pieces with a hacksaw and hid their remains under the floorboards in my living room."

Man says: "Oh, I only watch documentaries on television."
Translation: "I am totally addicted to reality television, but I'm too ashamed to admit it."

Man says: "I'm straight."
Translation: "I'm straight, but I watched *Brokeback Mountain*, and it gave me a tingly sensation in my crotch that made me long to herd sheep in the mountains with a strapping young man wearing tight jeans and a ten-gallon hat."

Man says: "I've been single for a while, but only because I'm real picky."
Translation: "No one likes me, and I can't get a date."

Man says: "Oh, I'm exploring my career options."
Translation: "I'm unemployed."

Man says: "Um. My aunt is in the hospital so I may get a call and have to leave."

Translation: "I'm not sure if I'm going to be able to stick this out with you."

Man says: "So, what do you look for in a guy?"
Translation: "What about *me* will you find totally charming?"

Man says: "What did you like least about your last boyfriend?"
Translation: "What parts of my personality should I conceal from you?"

Man says: "I got this scar in a bar fight."
Translation: "I got this scar from walking into a door."

Man says: "I hope you're enjoying your meal."
Translation: "Any chance I can eat whatever you don't? I mean, I paid for it and all."

Man says: "Let's go to your place."
Translation: "I don't think you want to make love on my *Star Wars* sheets."

Man says: "Let's have dessert."
Translation: "You're not half bad."

Man says: "Check please."
Translation: "I'm done with this date."

Man says: "Waiter! Another bottle of wine, please."
Translation: "I don't want to remember any of this tomorrow."

Man says: "Ah, here comes the check."
Translation: "Let me see if you're going to pull out your wallet."

Man says: "I'll pass on dessert. I'm on a diet."
Translation: "I can't afford this bill."

How to Turn Man Off

Sometimes tourists spend so much time running around seeing all the sights of their host country that they find themselves utterly exhausted at the end of the day. And the last thing they want to do is engage in lovemaking. So, if you find yourself the target of Man's unwanted amorous overtures, here are a few ways to turn Mr. Pointer into Mr. Floppy in no time:

1. Shave your pubic hair to resemble the face of Man's mother
2. Wear Old Spice
3. Tell Man you really want a baby
4. Grow out your armpit hair and stop using deodorant
5. Talk about your feelings
6. Ask Man to talk about his feelings
7. Drench your naked body in nonalcoholic beer foam
8. Tell Man you have a headache
9. Put a framed photograph of your mother on the bedside table
10. Tell Man you're ovulating, allergic to latex, and went off the Pill

End of First Date Manspeak

So, you got through the strained conversation of the first date and managed to snarf down the entire dessert. Now it's time to part ways. But you don't know what Man is thinking. Does he want a second date? Sex? Or to never call you again. No worries! Man will indicate his wishes with a series of gestures and words—you just have to know what to look and listen for.

Man says: "We should do this again soon."
Translation: "We should do this again tomorrow while I still remember your name."

Man says: "Let me walk you to your door."
Translation: "Let me walk you to your bedroom."

Man says: "Gee, it's a bit nippy out here on the porch."
Translation: "Having your tongue down my throat would really warm things up."

Man says: "How about we take in a movie?"
Translation: "I have nothing to say to you . . . and am jonesing for some Goobers."

Man says: (with a yawn) "Well, I've got an early morning, so I should probably be getting home."
Translation: "The best part of this date was the appetizer."

Man says: "Give me your home number, your work number, your cell number."
Translation: "I'm definitely going to call you."

Man says: "And your email address."
Translation: "I'm going to send you tons and tons of computer virus warnings for the rest of your life."

Man says: "I'll give you my phone number."
Translation: "I'll give you a fake number and breathe a sigh of relief that you can't reach me ever again."

Man says: "Well, it was nice meeting you."
Translation: "Well, it's nice knowing this date is over."

Man says: "I insist on driving you home."
Translation: "I'm driving a rental car and want to take advantage of the unlimited mileage."

Man says: "I hope you enjoyed your dinner."
Translation: "I'd say I earned a smooch, wouldn't you?"

Man says: "Here's a stick of gum."
Translation: "I'm going to kiss you."

Man says: "It's a beautiful night for a walk."
Translation: "I really don't want to pay for your cab."

Man says: "Wow! Look at the time!"
Translation: "Wow! You've got really bad breath."

Man says: "Can I come in for a minute?"
Translation: "I have to pee like a race horse, and I'll bet your bathroom is way cleaner than mine."

Man says: "Hmmm. This rain makes driving treacherous."
Translation: "You can get yourself home, right?"

Man says: "Sure, I'll call you."
Translation: "You stand as much a chance of hearing from me again as you do of getting a call from Jimmy Hoffa."

Man says: "I had a really good time tonight."
Translation: "You're not half as dull as you look."

Manland Gifts and What They Mean

When tourists arrive in Hawaii they are greeted by beautiful hula dancers who give them flowery leis to wear around their necks. When tourists arrive in Japan they are given tiny cups filled with lethal doses of sake. Well, when you arrive in Manland you don't get anything.

But as you get to know the inhabitants of this fascinating country, it is not uncommon to receive gifts of some sort from a particularly gracious host. This is yet another way Man attempts to gain a female tourist's affection . . . or at least, gain access to a female tourist's undergarments. And these gifts speak volumes about Man's personality. Know the facts.

Flowers

They smell good. They look pretty. And they say so much . . . ah, but what exactly do they say?

1. *A single rose:* "I totally forgot about this special occasion, but luckily, the hot dog vendor was giving these away with every bun."

2. *A bouquet of carnations:* "I felt compelled to buy you something so I don't look like a creep, and these were in my budget."

3. *A dozen short-stemmed roses just budding:* "I really like you, but not enough to pay twice as much to get you the ones with long stems that you and I both know you'll only cut the stems off of anyway so the flowers will fit in the vase."

4. *A dozen short-stemmed roses in full bloom:* "I really like you, and I went to a special florist to get you these so they are in perfect bloom this evening when we make love."

5. *A dozen short-stemmed roses with a few withering petals:* "I really like you, and I went to a special florist to get you these, but then I left them in the car overnight by accident."

6. *A dozen long-stemmed roses just budding:* "I think I'm falling in love with you."

7. *A dozen long-stemmed roses in full bloom:* "I know I'm falling in love with you."

8. *A dozen long-stemmed roses with a few withering petals:* "I thought I was in love with you, but it sort of freaked me out, so I'm pulling away a bit to think on it and hope you'll just leave me alone for a few days."

9. *A dozen long-stemmed roses with a card attached addressed to another woman:* "Ooops."

Jewelry

It's shiny. It's expensive. And it says, "I'm thinking about you." But what exactly is Man thinking about you?

1. *Plastic ring from a vending machine:* "I thought this was just gonna be a one-night stand—not sure how to get outta this. Hoping this does the trick."

2. *Sea shell necklace:* "I went on vacation without you, but remembered to pick this up."

3. *Silver-plated football pendant:* "If we're going to get serious, I need you to get serious about my interests."

4. *Silver-plated pendant with your initial:* "I know your name begins with this letter . . . and that's about all I know about you."

5. *A charm bracelet with no charms on it:* "You're charming, but I'm still not sure how much I like you."

6. *The classic gold heart pendant:* "I like you a lot, but I still don't know who you are so I just bought this thing because it was on sale in the display case."

7. *Classic gold heart pendant with your birthstone in it:* "I like you enough to not only remember your birthday, but to check to see which birthstone represents it."

8. *18k gold pendant with cubic zirconium chip without initials:* "I think you're really pretty and really smart, and I think I could be serious about you, but I hope to God you can't tell this isn't a real diamond."

9. *18k gold pendant with cubic zirconium chip with initials:* "I like you, but I also worry that you may not be smart enough to remember your own initials, so here they are in case you ever suffer from amnesia."

10. *18k gold pendant with diamond chip with personal engraving:* "I'm really serious about you, and you'd better start doing that sex thing we talked about because this cost a lot of money."

11. *Something from his mother's jewelry collection:* "I'm

seriously thinking of asking you to marry me, but if we break up, I want this back."

Miscellaneous

They're generic. They're impersonal. . . . Ah, but are they really?

1. *Windshield scraper:* "I'm not planning on sticking around much longer, but I care enough about you to fear for your safety during the winter months of the year."
2. *Hat and scarf set:* "I think of you as a sister, and I don't care for your hairdo at all."
3. *The standard teddy bear:* "I don't have much imagination and really haven't gotten to know you as a person, but I'm capable of becoming a more creative person—so please give me the chance."
4. *A scented candle:* "I want to run my hands all over your body and make you feel things you've never felt before . . . while saving on my electricity bill."
5. *Fruit basket:* "Someone gave this to me, and I have no use for it. By the way, I may be gay."
6. *Sausage of the Month Club membership:* "I am definitely gay."
7. *CD you already have:* "I am trying to be thoughtful but don't bother noticing anything about your personal tastes whatsoever."
8. *CD of band you hate, but he loves:* "I want to be with you, but I need incentive."
9. *Round-trip single ticket to Jamaica:* "I think you're a little stressed, but I care about you, and I want this to

work, so I'm sending you on a vacation so you can regroup and come back more likeable."

10. *All-expenses-paid vacation for two to Jamaica:* "I'm serious about you and want us to take this trip together . . . I also need to do a drug run."

11. *One-way single ticket to Jamaica:* (No surprise here.) "I want you to move to Jamaica and never come back."

CHAPTER FIVE

Mating Rituals of Manland

Don't have sex, man. It leads to kissing and
pretty soon you have to start talking to them.
—Steve Martin

Tourists visiting a foreign country often have special needs that must be met. A wheelchair-bound tourist to Paris needs a hotel outfitted with access ramps. A vegetarian tourist in Germany needs steamed vegetables rather than bratwurst available on her room service menu. And really unathletic people visiting the Swiss Alps need really patient ski instructors to greet them on the slopes so they don't tumble to their deaths in a blizzard of white powder. And you? You too have special needs while in Manland. And those needs come in the form of a slight twitching sensation in your nether regions that signifies your need to make mad passionate love with one of the locals so you can go home and brag that you got laid.

But before exchanging bodily fluids with any of the natives, you have to do some research. Just as you wouldn't trek into the Yucatán jungle without bringing some bug spray and a book that tells you which spiders can kill and which spiders just look like they can kill, you cannot possibly go out in search of the ultimate orgasm without knowing the basics about Manland sex.

The History of Manland Sex

The continent of Manland lays claim to one of the most plentiful populations in the world, boasting such a high ratio of citizens per square foot of land that it makes China and India look as vacant as the Bates Hotel in the off season. Throughout history, while minuscule specks in the universe like Nauru and Tuvalu struggled fruitlessly to propel their respective populations to new heights, Manland's inhabitancy rate simply could not stop multiplying. This was due to Man's ceaseless engagement in coitus, an irrepressible urge stemming from his constant fear of annihilation by encroaching neighboring countries. As a result, ancient Man operated on the belief that the way to ensure the staying power of the male civilization was to constantly stick his hoo-hoo into ancient Woman's hoo-ha and produce little Men. And so he did. And so the population boomed.

Eventually, Manland's reputation as an established world power was realized, and the pressure to procreate was off. With the advent of condoms, the Pill, and the vasectomy, Man discovered that coitus served an additional purpose: It simply felt damn good! Soon sex in Manland was more for recreational purposes than anything else. And that's why the rituals of Manland sex are harder for Woman to comprehend than Einstein's theory of relativity.

Sexual Positions and What They Mean

Just as reaching the top of the Eiffel Tower is the ultimate take-home experience for a trip to Paris, one of the highlights of a voyage to Manland is experiencing fornication with a local. It is a badge of honor for a female tourist to come home having taken a pleasurable ride on the Manland train of love.

But the world of Man Sex is as perplexing as the recipe for Twinkies. Man uses sex very differently from the way Woman does. While those of us fortunate enough to be of the female gender tend to draw on sex to express deep feelings of appreciation for another human being, Man likes to have sex because well, it feels good and helps pass the time.

Making sense of sexual positions in Manland is a useful tool while moseying about these alien environs in search of a memorable orgasm. To ensure your experience with Manland sex is a good one, familiarize yourself with the rules of coital engagement.

Each sexual position that Man tries to thrust upon you reveals a great deal about Man and his intentions. The sooner you can translate his suggestion of dressing you up as an elf and suspending you from the ceiling fan into emotional terms, the quicker you can decide if this is a tourist attraction you are interested in standing on line to see.

Doggy style (also known as the Bone/the Fido/the Canus Retreat): Man wants to have sex, but not necessarily with you.
Missionary style (also known as the Poke/the Lazy Way/the Partial Nap): Man wants to be able to kiss you while you make love, but worries you are heavier than you look.

You on top: (also known as the Corkscrew): Man wants to give you the best orgasm of your life, but wants to tweak your nipples if he gets bored waiting for you to finish.

The spooning position (also known as the Stuck on You): Man wants to make love slowly and passionately, but doesn't want to have to be fully awake.

Reverse doggy style with you wearing a strap-on (also known as the Open Mind): Man is seriously questioning his sexuality.

You on your back on the kitchen table with your legs over Man's shoulders (also known as the Dinner Bell): Man wants to be able to look in your eyes as he orgasms, and then grab a light snack afterward.

On the floor (also known as the Sweep): Man is in the mood for hard sex and his sheets have dust mites in them.

69 (also known as the Yin Yang): Man is such a peaceful creature he wants to make love to you mimicking the Yin Yang symbol.

You handcuffed to the bedpost (also known as the Perp/the Hostage): Man is afraid you will leave him.

Man arrives in bed with a pet hamster (also known as the Rodent): Man just joined PETA.

You bent over his office desk (also known as Overtime): Man is "behind" in his work.

Against the wall, standing up, fully clothed (also known as Custer's Last Stand): Man is so overcome with desire for you he cannot wait to have you . . . also, he needs help hanging that picture that keeps going crooked above your head.

You on top, but facing toward Man's feet (also known as the Reverse Corkscrew): Man is in love with the silhouette of

your backside in the moonlight . . . and would like you to
give him a foot massage.

Up against the wall, from behind (also known as the
Squished Face): Man is horny, but thinks you have bad
breath.

Sex Manspeak

Remember that time you and your girlfriend took a crash
course in Spanish and then flew off to Puerto Rico to practice
what you had learned? But when you got to San Juan and tried
to speak in the proper Spanish you had studied, no one knew
what the heck you were saying? That's because you weren't using the local dialect. Most foreign-language-speaking countries
have them—odd little variations on the native language that
are used by inhabitants of particular regions.

Once Man has sex on his mind, not only does his body un-
dergo some very obvious changes, but his speech alters as well.
After a considerable amount of slurring, Man inevitably slips
into an ancient and horny dialect that has been around for centuries called Sex Manspeak. This vernacular is entirely different from regular Manspeak, and, just to confuse you, contains
three ancient subdialects; Precoital, Intracoital, and Postcoital
Manspeak. If there is even the slightest chance that you will be
dropping your drawers for Man, commit the translations of all
three of these foreign dialects to memory. They will come in
handy (no pun intended) more than you can imagine, and keep
you from getting screwed while you're getting screwed.

Precoital Manspeak

Precoital Manspeak is used during the Evaluation Stage of Manland sex. It is the dialect with which Man communicates when he is in the process of assessing his chances with you. Every question he poses is secretly designed to determine exactly how far you will go, and what you are willing to do when you get there. The goal of Precoital Manspeak is to charm you. Lull you into a false sense of security. Weaken your defenses. Well, Man may think he is cleverly disguising that singular goal of his (to see your hoo-ha). But he is soooo not!

Man says: "Let me give you a hug."
Translation: "Lemme see if your boobs are real."

Man says: "Why don't we just have a seat on the couch for a minute, shall we?"
Translation: "This couch is long enough for me to get you flat on your back in about three-point-six seconds."

Man says: "Your hair smells terrific."
Translation: "This is good. No signs of body odor."

Man says: "I want to take this slowly."
Translation: "I'll count to three before I grab your left breast."

Man says: "I really care about you."
Translation: "I really care about you naked."

Man says: "I feel such a connection with you."
Translation: "I feel the need to connect my penis to your vagina."

Man says: "Allergic to anything?"
Translation: "Allergic to latex?"

Man says: "I just need to take these er . . . vitamins first."
Translation: "I hope you didn't see the word *Viagra* on these pills."

Man says: "I wear a size-twelve shoe."
Translation: "I am hung like a Clydesdale."

Man says: "I haven't been with someone in a long time."
Translation: "I haven't been with someone since yesterday."

Man says: "That's a pretty necklace."
Translation: "I can't stop staring at your boobs."

Man says: "You seem like a really strong, authoritative woman, and I find that so attractive."
Translation: "I wonder if you'd be willing to dress up in leather head to toe and whip me?"

Man says: "Can you hand me that pillow, please?"
Translation: "Shoot! I have a boner!"

Man says: "Is that a cold sore on your lip?"
Translation: "OH MY GOD! IS THAT HERPES???"

Man says: "Let me pour you another drink."
Translation: "The less sober you are, the more chance I have at this."

Man says: "Unlike other guys, I'm not just interested in sex."
Translation: "Just like other guys—I am only interested in sex."

Man says: "You've probably dated a lot of men?"
Translation: "How many STDs have you contracted in the last year?"

Man says: "It's warm in here; I'm going to turn down the heat a bit."
Translation: "I can almost see your nipples through that shirt."

Man says: "So, um, are you part Italian?"
Translation: "You look like you have a lot of body hair."

Man says: "Do you feel comfortable with me?"
Translation: "Do you feel comfortable enough to do things on camera with me?"

Man says: "I've only been with three other women."
Translation: "I've been with three thousand other women and just left off a few zeroes."

Man says: "I could just sit and talk with you for hours."
Translation: "I could just sit and talk with you for hours . . . as long as I know there is sex at the end."

Man says: "No, I've never had a homosexual experience."
Translation: "No, I've never had a homosexual experience that I'll admit to."

Man says: "I don't want to pressure you . . ."
Translation: "I'm giving you five more minutes before I'm outta here."

Man says: "I just want to lie here with you and feel you breathe."
Translation: "If I get you in the horizontal position, it's easier to undo your pants."

Man says: "Let's go into the kitchen for a snack."
Translation: "I'm a complete psycho and do disgusting things with kitchen appliances."

Man says: "I'm really interested in getting to know you."
Translation: "I'm really interested in getting to know you naked."

Intracoital Manspeak

Once you have given Man the green light in the boudoir, Man slips into the second stage of Sex Manspeak: Intracoital Manspeak. He breaks into this dialect the moment the underwear comes off and the birth control comes out. Intracoital Manspeak is about Man concealing his er, shortcomings, and building up his prowess. No matter how many tourists he has ridden the merry-go-round with, Man has no idea what you, this new and very intimidating tourist, like and don't like in bed. So everything he says during this sweaty and bumpy interim is designed to feel you out . . . while feeling you up.

Snappy Retorts

Once in a while Man will say something so rude, so offensive, so thoroughly insensitive after sex that you simply cannot, and should not, let it slide. This is one of those times:

Man says: "I'd like to spend the night, but I have to get up early in the morning."

You respond: "Yeah, and I'd like to give you oral sex, but I have to get up early in the morning."

Man says: "I want to be as close to you as possible."
Translation: "Let's not use a condom."

Man says: "So, is your period pretty regular?"
Translation: "You're on the Pill, right?"

Man says: "That's quite a birthmark you have."
Translation: "Crap! Is that what a genital wart looks like?

Man says: "I have carpal tunnel syndrome."
Translation: "I can't get your bra undone for the life of me."

Man says: "Your breasts are amazing."
Translation: "How much did these things cost?"

Man says: "I'm not really into blow jobs."
Translation: "Your teeth look really sharp."

Man says: "Would you excuse me for a second?"
Translation: "I have to go use that pump thing I ordered off the Internet."

Man says: "Maybe we shouldn't rush into this."
Translation: "I'm nervous as hell."

Man says: "Keep your boots on. It's sexy."
Translation: "Your feet stink."

Man says: "I'm so hot for you, let's skip the foreplay."
Translation: "I wish you had shaved your legs."

Man says: "It's a bit chilly in here, isn't it?"
Translation: "My penis is really small."

Man says: "Let's do it in the shower."
Translation: "Your armpits smell."

Man says: "Let's turn off the lights."
Translation: "I have a really hairy mole on my back that I don't want you to see."

Man says: "Wow, your dog is really friendly."
Translation: "Please tell your dog to stop licking my butt."

Man says: "Just close your eyes and relax."
Translation: "Stop staring at me. It's making me nervous."

Man says: "Oh, I want you on top of me, baby."
Translation: "Geez, this missionary position is killing my arms!"

Man says: "Does this feel good?"
Translation: "Make some noise so I know you're alive, woman!"

Man says: "Let's take a break."
Translation: "I think I pulled my groin muscle."

Man says: "I like making love in the quiet of the night."
Translation: "Could you not talk so much during this?"

Man says: "Do you smell something?"
Translation: "Did you fart?"

Man says: "I'm thirsty."
Translation: "I have a pubic hair stuck in my throat."

Man says: "I love you so much."
Translation: "Oh, *please* swallow . . . *please* swallow."

Man says: "Um, so, what do you think of the national economy these days?"
Translation: "I'm going to come if I don't focus on something else right now."

Man says: "I think I heard the doorbell ring."
Translation: "Could you hurry it up a bit? My tongue is getting tired."

Man says: "Oh, yeah, baby, you know you wanna come."
Translation: "Why is this taking so long?"

Man says: "Call me Dick."
Translation: "Talk dirty to me, baby."

Man says: "Yes! Yes! Yes!"
Translation: "Yes! Yes! Yes!"

Postcoital Manspeak

After you and Man have had fun violating each other's bodies (and probably a few international laws as well) you will witness the final stage of Sex Manspeak: Postcoital Manspeak. Better known as the Performance-Oriented Stage, this is the period of time at which Man is most vulnerable. He is physically spent, intellectually confused, and emotionally insecure.

Everything Man says is an attempt to find out what you thought of his performance and do damage control for any area in which he may have failed. Ladies, it's not a pretty picture. And this stage is usually the reason we end up going at it again with Man: to give him a second chance.

Man says: "Was it good for you?"
Translation: "How do I stack up compared to your other partners?"

Man says: "So, what's your stand on abortion?"
Translation: "Um, the condom broke."

Man says: "Wow, that was amazing."
Translation: "Wow, I was amazing."

Man says: "It's dangerous for a woman to overexert herself."
Translation: "You've got to be kidding, That's all I've got!"

Man says: "You sure made a lot of noise back there."
Translation: "Were you faking it?"

Man says: "Let's do it again."
Translation: "I think I screwed up that last part."

Man says: "So, you and your girlfriends. You talk about personal stuff?"
Translation: "When you tell them about this, how big are you going to say my penis was?"

Man says: "I liked that thing you did with your tongue."
Translation: "I'd like you to do that thing you did with your tongue to me again . . . right now."

Man says: "That was incredible."
Translation: "Anytime I can stick my penis in something, it's incredible."

Man says: "Huh, this bed is a bit small."
Translation: "You need to lose some weight, honey."

Man says: "I'm gonna hop in the shower."
Translation: "I don't cuddle."

Man says: "I can't stay, I have to get up early in the morning."
Translation: "Yikes! You looked attractive when I was drunk!"

Man says: "I'll call you."
Translation: "I'll call you if I test positive for anything."

CHAPTER SIX

Extending Your Stay

*You cannot travel the path until you become
the path itself.*
—Hindu prince Guatama Siddartha

So, you've explored the major districts in Manland. Taken in all the famous sights, dined on the tantalizing cuisine, and even gotten to know the locals (some biblically). You think back to the time you traveled to Alaska, when, after you'd had your fill of whale blubber and glaciers, you were ready to head home. Heck, you couldn't wait to get back to the comforts of your own land. But oddly, as your visit to Manland draws to a close, you feel a lump in your throat. A skip in your heartbeat. A twitch in your nether regions. Why? Because you've fallen in love with one of the inhabitants, that's why!

Yes, despite Man's odd behavior, despite the disturbing cultural customs and belief systems to which this creature subscribes, you want nothing more than to see this Man a bit more. Date him. Yes, you have decided to extend your visa to see if this Man has long-range potential.

Well, this is all really romantic, honey, but there are a few

113

things you should know before you postpone that return flight back to the Motherland, and begin bragging to all your friends that you're dating a foreigner.

Just as cute little tiger cubs grow into giant man-eaters with short tempers and long claws, Man becomes quite a different person once Woman has infiltrated his world. He gains weight, demonstrates particularly offensive habits that weren't apparent a few days ago, and begins communicating in yet another series of ancient Manland dialects designed to confuse you.

But if you are really enjoying your time in Manland, and want to stay a bit longer to get to know Man better, more power to you. Just know what you're getting yourself into. And how to get yourself out of it!

Not Quite Boyfriend Manspeak

He's a boyfriend in the sense that he knows your hotel number by heart and brings you flowers every time he sees you. He spends every waking minute with you, helps you convert your Manland currency, and has introduced you to all his friends at the local watering hole. And yet, this new so-called boyfriend has yet to invite you to meet his parents, or let you leave a single item of clothing at his place. Clearly he likes you too much to dump you, but not quite enough to commit your tube of Vagisil to his medicine chest. He wants to be there for you— he's just not sure how much. Not knowing what this Man is saying can make assimilating into the male culture quite difficult. And seeing as all the experts say communication is the key to the success of a committed relationship, God help you, Woman, if you hadn't picked up this book!

This is a confusing time for Man as he attempts to do what

Man has never been able to do: get in touch with his feelings. Thus, the patois with which this hairy ball of confusion expresses himself can be baffling for a visitor to the Not-Quite-Dating region of Manland.

Man says: "My bed's too small to sleep two comfortably."
Translation: "You know the rules: We have sex, then you go home."

Man says: "I can't move out, my mom is very attached to me."
Translation: "I'm very attached to not having to pay rent."

Man says: "I think I'm coming down with something."
Translation: "I have another chick coming over in a bit."

Man says: "It's a good idea for you to have your own place in case my place burns down in an unexpected fire."
Translation: "You are *not* moving in with me!"

Man says: "Sorry. I forgot to call you last night."
Translation: "I totally remembered to call you, but just didn't."

Man says: "I love . . . watching movies with you."
Translation: "I feel this little pang in my heart when you're not around, but am not sure I want to admit that I may be falling in love with you."

Man says: "Vacation? How about we just go somewhere for the day?"
Translation: "I can only take you in small doses."

Man says; "I'd love to meet your parents sometime."
Translation: "I am going to keep saying this until we break up, or they die."

Man says: "Sure I'd like to go away for the weekend with you to Amish country."
Translation: "I'll wait until the last minute, then call you and pretend I have the flu."

Man says: "I'd let you drive, but my car's been making a funny noise."
Translation: "You're never going to get behind the wheel of my car."

Man says: "Oh, 'love.' It's such a subjective word, don't you think?"
Translation: "Love means I have to watch you get old and fat."

Man says: "I can't afford call waiting."
Translation: "If I get call waiting, then you can always reach me."

Man says: "I am fond of you."
Translation: "I like you too much to dump you, but not enough to move in with you."

Man says: "Why don't we stay at your place tonight?"
Translation: "I need to be able to leave when I want."

Man says: "I don't really have anything in the fridge."
Translation: "Please don't drink my beer."

Man says: "That tattoo is just henna, right?"
Translation: "Please tell me you didn't permanently ink my name into your skin!"

Man says: "Oh, it'll warm up soon, honey."
Translation: "If I give you my coat, it would mean you own a piece of me."

Man says: "I'm seeing my ex for lunch."
Translation: "I need to see if I made the right choice in dumping her for you."

Man says: "You are the only woman for me."
Translation: "You seem to be the only woman for me, but I'll keep looking."

Man says: "I love being with you."
Translation: "I love being with you sometimes."

Man says: "Gee, I'd be happy to let you use my credit card, but I don't have one."
Translation: "You could be one of those people who steal identities."

Man says: "I don't think I can go to your friend's wedding on Saturday."
Translation: "I don't want you getting any ideas."

Man says: "Hey, I'm just calling to tell you that you left your hair clip at my place."
Translation: "I miss you."

Man says: "Sorry. My medicine chest is really packed."
Translation: "You are *so* not leaving your toothbrush here."

Man says: "Can I have the remote back, please?"
Translation: "Oh my god! I'm losing control of my life!"

Man says: "Define 'long-term' . . ."
Translation: "Aw, crap, what have I gotten myself into?"

Man says: "Instead of a puppy, how 'bout we adopt a fourteen-year-old stray?"
Translation: "I can only guarantee a commitment of like, six months or so."

Snappy Retorts

Once in a while Not-Quite-Committed Man cuts through the malarkey and tells you the way it is. He is banking on the fact that you will appreciate his honesty. Should you be on the receiving end of such "honesty," be "honest" right back. (Do it for Womankind!)

Not-Quite-Committed Man says: "I guess I'm just not ready to commit to you."
You respond: "Oh yeah? Then I guess I'm just not ready to commit to giving you sex."

Man says: "Wow! You sure carry a lot of stuff in your
   purse."
Translation: "Oh, God. Looks like you've packed enough to
   stay the week."

Man says: "My parents are dead."
Translation: "My parents are alive and well and living in
   Wisconsin, but you're never gonna meet them."

Breaking-Up Manspeak

Perhaps you violated the rules of sharing a living space with
Man. Or maybe your seemingly enjoyable existence ended up
infringing on Man's boys-night-out rituals. Who knows what
went wrong in his mind, but whatever it was, Man has decided
you're not his cup of tequila. He is ending your affair and asking you to leave this place you have started to call home.

Being dumped by Man is like being presented with a beau-
tifully wrapped gift of steaming dog poop. He will pad his re-
jection of you with words so soft, so seemingly nice and
self-deprecating, not because Man has a conscience . . . but because he doesn't want to spend hours consoling a weeping
tourist begging for a second chance. And he doesn't want a
public scene either. So, Man will do everything in his power to
make the breakup seem as though it is not your fault. That he
is "doing you a favor." Get real. Don't let the polite phrasing
he'll employ fool you. If your new Man utters any of the following phrases, walk away before you waste any more of your
precious time on this loser.

Man says (on the phone): "Let's meet in the public square at high noon."
Translation: "Let's meet where there are a lot of people around, including a high level of police presence, so you can't kill me."

Man says: "We need to talk."
Translation: "I need to talk, and you need to keep quiet."

Man says: "It's not you, it's me."
Translation: "It's you, not me."

Man says: "There's no one else."
Translation: "There's someone else."

Man says: "I'm just not ready to commit."
Translation: "The sex is getting boring."

Man says: "I'll come by your house tomorrow to make sure you're okay."
Translation: "I need to pick up my CDs."

Man says: "It's better this way."
Translation: "It's better for me this way."

Man says: "I think we should see other people."
Translation: "I think I should see other people, and you should not see anyone ever again and instead, sit at home and pine away for me for the rest of your life because it'll make me feel like a tough guy."

Man says: "I hate to do this so close to your birthday."
Translation: "This is saving me soooo much money!"

Man says: "I just need some space."
Translation: "You are smothering me."

Man says: "I need to find myself."
Translation: "I need to find myself naked with another
   woman."

Man says: "Things just aren't working out between us."
Translation: "You're more annoying than I thought you'd be."

Man says: "You're too good for me."
Translation: "I'm too good for you."

Man says: "I'm just not ready to settle down yet."
Translation: "I'm just not ready to settle down with you yet."

Man says: "I'll miss your smile the most."
Translation: "I'll miss the free sex the most."

Man says: "I hope we can still be friends."
Translation: "I have no intention of ever speaking to you
   again."

Man says: "I'll always love you."
Translation: "I'll always love your dog."

Man says: "Call me if you need anything."
Translation: "I'll be screening my calls."

CHAPTER SEVEN

Applying for Citizenship

*When you see a married couple walking
down the street, the one that's a few steps
ahead is the one that's mad.*

—Helen Rowland

Just as only a very few propitious vacationers to Scotland will return from their retreat having spotted the famously elusive Loch Ness Monster, it is a rare but much celebrated occasion when a female visitor to Manland is invited to apply for citizenship. This means she has successfully assimilated into one of the most elusive cultures on the planet and is considered a valuable enough commodity to invest in.

But just as every international airport throughout the world requires arriving visitors to pass through an extensive screening with a Customs agent, Man does not hand out an application for citizenship before doing a serious background check. After all, he is about to forsake the purchase of a sports car in order to buy you an overpriced diamond ring. So, it only stands to reason that before he lets you into his world, he needs to gather vital information about you. Data that will enable him to assess exactly what kind of Manland inhabitant you will make. Confirm that you are worthy of a green card.

And so comes the Manland Naturalization Test—a clever system of investigative tactics Man draws from to see if you can, in fact, be incorporated into his society. This coordinated scheme of checks and balances is comprised of a series of intensive oral exams (no, not the kind you're thinking) which can be quite tough to pass. So, if you really want your green card . . . and that lovely diamond ring . . . study up!

The Oral Exams

The oral portion of your test for citizenship requires you to answer some seemingly random questions. The key to answering these queries correctly is *understanding* them. Not an easy task. Ever since that incident in the Garden of Eden when Woman disobeyed a direct order from her superiors, Man doesn't trust the whole commitment thing. He figures that, just like Eve, Modern Woman can turn on a dime and ruin his life. Thus, the verbal questions posed by the proctor during this examination period are designed to alert Man to any dangers that may be lurking in your system.

Ladies, the Manland Naturalization Test is an excruciatingly difficult undertaking. Harder than the SATs. But it *can* be aced. You just need to listen carefully to the questions and not make any stupid mistakes. The oral exam is broken up into three parts: the Considering Popping the Question Pop Quiz, the Popping the Question Pop Quiz, and the Bachelor Party Pop Quiz. Below are the test questions Man will most likely ask you, along with their translations, the suggested answer, and an explanation of why the answer works. These answers are designed to relax Man's defenses while simultaneously making an honest statement about yourself and what you expect out of this deal. Now, let's take a look at the test, shall we?

Oral Exam 1

The Considering Popping the Question Pop Quiz

This first stage of the oral exams is administered when Man is considering proposing to you. After all, he's not about to hand over his house key and surname to just any Woman. Manland has kept its gates closed to outsiders for centuries. So, the sentinels guarding these gates must be assured that anyone passing through security can be trusted to respect this community. If the wrong interloper slips through the cracks, as Adam found out many years ago, all hell will break loose. (In Adam's case, quite literally.)

Applying for citizenship is a serious undertaking, but if you pass this first round, you're one step closer to some bling-bling on your left hand!

Man says: "Would you like to browse through that really expensive jewelry store for a minute?"

Translation: "Let's see if I can afford to marry you."

Suggested answer: "Why don't we go to a sports bar first and talk about our options?"

Why this answer works: This shows Man that you expect him to demonstrate good taste and get you a really nice ring, but are willing to let him take his time in picking it out.

Man says: "So, what do you think of Joan Rivers's new look?"

Translation: "How far will you go to keep from aging badly?"

Suggested answer: "I'm all for plastic surgery if it makes a woman feel better about herself, but frankly, I'd never let myself go in the first place."

Why this answer works: This shows Man that you understand his appreciation for beauty, and will do what you can, within reason, to continue piquing his interest for a long time.

Man says: "Are any of your girlfriends bisexual?"

Translation: "Are any of your girlfriends willing to have a threesome once this thing between us starts getting dull?"

Suggested answer: "Some of them are, but mostly because they haven't figured out how to satisfy a man."

Why this answer works: This puts an end to Man's stupid little fantasy before it's even fully formulated, but does so without making you appear susceptible to jealous rages.

Man says: "Why don't you let me drive?"

Translation: "I fear for my life when Woman is behind the wheel."

Suggested answer: "Sure thing, honey. I'll drive on the way back."

Why this answer works: You are humoring Man's innate fear of not being in control, while simultaneously reminding him that things won't always go his way.

Man says: "Want to watch that cooking show with me?"
Translation: "Your cooking sucks."
Suggested answer: "Sure. But how about we order in dinner after?"
Why this answer works: This show Man that you are willing to learn, but on your terms, not his.

Man says: "So, seems like you're pretty close with your parents, huh?"
Translation: "Chances are we'll do well in their will, huh?"
Suggested answer: "Yes. Incredibly close. And they've done so much for me with so little."
Why this answer works: This throws Man off the inheritance scent. The less he knows about what he stands to gain should you get eaten by a grizzly bear, the better. Man should be marrying for love, not for the house with the pool that he might get if your parents kick the bucket.

Man says: "So, are you good with kids?"
Translation: "So, are you interested in having kids?"
Suggested answer: "Any child born into a home with two loving parents is going to know it's loved."
Why this answer works: This answer reminds Man that parenting is a two-person job.

Man says: "Geez, those polygamist folks sure are weird, huh?"
Translation: "So I guess moving us to Utah and getting a second wife is out of the question?"
Suggested answer: "Yes, they're just as weird as those

Amazon women who stone their men to death for infidelity."

Why this answer works: This lets Man know that you consider polygamy cheating—if he needs two wives, then you need a boyfriend.

Man says: "Are your parents as eclectic as they seem?"
Translation: "Are your parents as bat-shit crazy as they seem?"
Suggested answer: "Yes, and they remind me so much of your folks!"
Why this answer works: The sooner you equate your wacko tribe to his, the sooner Man will learn to not pass judgment.

Man says: "I'd only want a prenup if you want a prenup."
Translation: "Oh, please, please, please want a prenup!"
Suggested answer: "Yes, it's probably a good idea that I protect that trust fund I have."
Why this answer works: This gently reminds Man that he may have more to lose than you. (Even if you aren't worth a dime, let him think you are for the rest of his life.)

Man says: "Has your mom put on a bit of weight lately?"
Translation: "Do thunder thighs run in your family?"
Suggested answer: "It's possible. Speaking of which, has your father's forehead expanded?"
Why this answer works: If Man plans to spend your marriage commenting on every flaw that comes with the natural aging process, he better be aware that two can play at that game.

Man says: "How important are anniversaries to you?"

Translation: "Am I going to have to buy you jewelry every year?"

Suggested answer: "About as important as blowjobs are to you."

Why this answer works: Man needs to know that marriage is a matter of give and take: you *give* him oral sex . . . and then *take* a nice bracelet.

Man says: "Just curious—does your father own any firearms?"

Translation: "If I cheat on you, what are the chances I'll end up dead?"

Suggested answer: "Yes, and he shoots to kill."

Why this answer works: Second only to communication, fear can be the key to a good marriage.

Man says: "I bet there are going to be nights when you'd just prefer I go out with the guys and give you a break, right?"

Translation: "I'll kill myself if I can't get drunk off my butt at least once a week to escape your presence."

Suggested answer: "Absolutely. Those are the nights I'll use to hang out with some of my exes."

Why this answer works: Man has a bad habit of thinking he's the only one in need of a social outlet. He may just rethink that whole poker night thing if he knows your history isn't quite so historic.

Oral Exam 2

The Popping the Question Pop Quiz

If you passed Oral Exam 1 with flying colors, it's on to the next round of questions.

The second phase of the Manland Naturalization Test is the Popping the Question Pop Quiz, administered when Man, on bended knee, presents you with a ring—the Manland equivalent of a temporary green card. Beware: The operative word here is *temporary*. Man can just as easily slip that ring back in his pocket as he can slip it onto your finger. One wrong move and you're out. Don't mess this up, Woman! It would be such a shame to have come this far and then, because you were too lazy to study, get deported back home.

Man says: "Let's go to someplace private."

Translation: "I might change my mind at the last minute and need a quick escape route."

Suggested answer: "Sure. Somewhere well-lit, too, so I can see what you have in that box."

Why this answer Works: Man isn't the only one who might change his mind at the last minute. If that ring ain't big enough, you ain't stickin' around!

Man says: "Will you er . . . um . . . er . . . you know, marry me?"

Translation: "I just realized that you're the best I'm gonna do."

Suggested answer: "Let me think about it a moment."

Why this answer works: This tells Man that you, too, have your doubts, but leaves the lines open for negotiation.

Man says: "How do you feel about us growing old together?"

Translation: "How would you feel if I put you in a nursing home the minute you become a chore?"

Suggested answer: "I plan on being with you until the very end."

Why this answer works: This tells Man that, as far as you are concerned, marriage is for good. In health and in sickness . . . really, really old people sickness.

Man says: "You really want to invite your ex to the wedding?"

Translation: "You really want me to be forced to kill your ex in between the cocktails and appetizers?"

Suggested answer: "I'm sure you two can get along for one day."

Why this answer works: This tells Man that you respect the people in your past . . . and if he respects you, he'll have to do the same.

Man says: "You didn't want me to waste money on a really expensive ring, right?"

Translation: "I got this ring free with the purchase of a six-pack of beer at Costco. And now there's enough money left over to buy that HD television I've been eyeing."

Suggested answer: "I appreciate your instinct to economize and will do the same when your birthday rolls around."

Why this answer works: Man needs to know that saving money is a good thing . . . but saving money by shorting you isn't.

Man says: "You really think that wedding gown looks good on you?"

Translation: "That wedding gown costs too much."

Suggested answer: "This is the only one I would consider wearing, honey."

Why this answer works: For Woman, her wedding day is the Manland equivalent of seeing the Super Bowl live. A lifelong dream being realized. So, just as Man would spare no expense to get fifty-yardline seats to the game, you'll be damned if you'll skimp on your dress.

Man says: "How do you feel about keeping the wedding small?"

Translation: "Let's not invite any of your family."

Suggested answer: "The same way I feel about small penises."

Why this answer works: When Man marries you, he marries everyone in your life. The sooner he realizes that, the sooner you two will be on the same page.

Man says: "Do you really have to spend so much time planning this wedding?"

Translation: "Ask me one more question about this stupid wedding and I'm going to kill myself."

Suggested answer: "You're right. I have to stop obsessing. By the way, I'm going to be so tired on our honeymoon night, I think I'll just let what happens happen. If anything happens at all."

Why this answer works: If Man doesn't consider the details of the most important day of your life worth discussing, then let Man know that you're going to leave *everything* to chance.

> **Travel Tips: *Domesticating Man***
>
> Man will do anything to avoid doing the dishes. You must trick him into doing them. Try throwing your engagement ring down the sink so he has to go after it.

Oral Test 3

The Bachelor Party Pop Quiz

Congratulations! If you're reading this, you've passed the second phase of your Naturalization Test. This means you are that much closer to establishing permanent residency in Manland. But the night before you are sworn in as a new citizen is a pivotal testing period for Man. The bachelor party is an ancient ritual that has been observed since the dawn of Manland civilization. It is Man's last hurrah. His final night of freedom. The last time he can run around doing manly, sexist things like touching things he's not going to be allowed to touch anymore and licking things he's not going to be allowed to lick anymore. How you respond to the threat of this ritual—whether you subscribe to the "boys will be boys" adage, and leave Man be, or, in an attempt to squash his plans, force him to spend the night playing bingo with his mother, will give Man a bird's eye view into his future. The Bachelor Party Pop Quiz is Man's best chance to see exactly what you will bring to the table, and what you will take away from it.

And just so you know: if you fail this test, that ring you've been shining day and night? It gets revoked. Along with your temporary green card. Back on the plane you go!

Man says: "All right if the boys and I hang out a bit before the wedding tomorrow?"

Translation: "The boys and I are going to a bunch of strip clubs for lap dances. Then we're going to get drunk beyond comprehension, pick a bar fight or two, and hire some hookers to perform all sorts of unspeakable acts on our bodies."

Suggested answer: "Sure. I trust you."

Why this answer works: You are giving Man the space he needs, but reminding him that there are boundaries he needs to respect if he wants to live with a clean conscience.

Man says: "Can I borrow some singles for the vending machine?"

Translation: "I need singles for the stripper."

Suggested answer: "Sure. I'll go with you."

Why this answer works: Straight and to the point, this response forces Man to either fess up, or head out with no money for those strippers.

Man says: "How does my hair look?"

Translation: "How will other women think my hair looks?"

Suggested answer: "Let's just say I hope my boobs look as good as your hair does."

Why this answer works: This reminds Man that you are a hot commodity yourself, and that his opinion isn't the only one that matters.

Man says: "You don't care what time I get home, right?"
Translation: "I'm going to be home sometime tomorrow."
Suggested answer: "Come home whenever you like. I'm sure you'll check in with me throughout the evening."
Why this answer works. Man needs to know that he can have his freedom, but not disrespect you in the process.

Man says: "Honey, you know I wouldn't do anything that would upset you, don't you?"
Translation: "Honey, you know I wouldn't tell you about anything I did that would upset you, right?"
Suggested answer: "Of course, dear. But what we don't know about each other can't hurt."
Why this answer works: Man isn't the only one with secrets. And even if you don't have any, let him *think* you do.

Man says: "You know, I'm really not into these bachelor party things at all, right?"
Translation: "Man! I should get married more often!"
Suggested answer: "Then don't go. I don't want to see you suffer unnecessarily, dear."
Why this answer works: Man needs to learn to be true to his word. And his marriage vows.

Man says: "You know, I'll be thinking of you the whole time, right?"
Translation: "You'll be lucky if I remember your name when I get home."
Suggested answer: "Then maybe I should come with you?"
Why this answer works: Simple. It'll be fun to watch Man panic for a bit.

Man says: "Maybe we should push the wedding back a bit?"

Translation: "Oh, God, what was I thinking swearing off other women for the rest of my life?"

Suggested answer: "Whatever you're comfortable with. Hey, by the way, I'd like to feel like a virgin on my wedding night, so no sex until then, okay?"

Why this answer works: In one fell swoop you are telling Man that you have better things to do with your time than wait for him to make a decision. If you're not good enough for him to snap up right now? Then he's not good enough to take your clothes off for.

Man says: "All right if the guys and I just sit around and talk tonight?"

Translation: "All right if the guys and I just sit around really hot, really half-naked strippers and then talk about them all night?"

Suggested answer: "Sure. I think my girlfriends and I are going to do the same."

Why this answer works: Two can play at this game, pal.

Man says: "You believe me when I say I'm only going to have one beer, right?"

Translation: "I'm going to have one beer . . . after the fourteen shots of tequila."

Suggested answer: Just as much as you believe me when I say I'm on the Pill."

Why this answer works: The more Man knows you will match his little games point for point, the less likely he is to cheat.

Your Swearing-in Ceremony

If, by the time you reach this section of the book, you are still in possession of that temporary green card, congratulations! You passed your Manland Naturalization Test and are officially being welcomed as a guest citizen of this fascinating foreign land! You are one of the lucky expatriates from Womanland to get past the border patrol. No longer are you a stranger in a strange land . . . you are now a *legal resident* of a strange land.

The final stage of the naturalization process is being sworn in by an official of the Manland government. Most new inductees like to make a big deal out of this swearing-in procedure—so may we suggest that you invite lots of guests and hire a caterer to prepare plateloads of rubbery chicken and wet salmon entrees, and a three-tiered cake that looks better than it tastes. Oh, and don't forget the really bad cover bands playing really bad '80s music. And that dress you'll wear that looks like toilet paper. Sort of tacky. But overall, the event can be a great deal of fun. (And you get presents, to boot!)

The Swearing-in Oath

Once the guests have been seated and your drunken Uncle Charlie has been escorted out to the parking lot until the cops arrive, an officiant of the Manland government will swear you in. This is an exciting moment. But don't get so swept up in the pomp and circumstance that you fail to read between the lines. As you listen to Man's oath, make sure you can honestly and truly live with what you are about to get into, because once you're a citizen, that's it. There's no turning back. At least not without getting the government involved.

The Man Vows

BEFORE THESE WITNESSES (most of whom I have never met, and couldn't name if I had to) I vow to love you and care for you (unless you are puking, because that's just gross) as long as we both shall live (until you die, or I get bored). I take you with all your faults and strengths (but hope there are more strengths than faults) as I offer myself to you with my faults and strengths (and trust me, there are a lot of faults). I promise to help you when you need help (as long as you don't need help during football, hockey, baseball, or basketball season), and likewise, promise to turn to you when I need help (getting dressed in the morning because I still don't get the whole color coordination thing). I choose you as the person with whom I will spend the rest of my God-given life (and if you end up getting fat or hairy in certain places, I hope that life is a short one). With this ring (that cost way too much and looked so much bigger in the store) I thee wed.

The Woman Vows (This is Your Part, Ditz!)

BEFORE THESE WITNESSES (most of whom are my guests because I have way more friends than you do) I vow to love you and care for you (unless you have erectile dysfunction) as long as we both shall live (or until you die, or I get bored). I take you with all your faults and strengths (but am fairly certain there are more faults than strengths) as I offer myself to you with my faults and strengths (and trust me, there are like, no faults). I promise to help you when you need help (as long as you put the dishes in the dishwasher and walk the dog when it's cold), and likewise, promise to turn to you when I need help (touching up my roots). I choose you as the person with whom I will spend the rest of my God-given life (and if you end up getting fat or going bald, I hope that life is a short one). With this ring (that isn't at all what I wanted) I thee wed.

The Manland officiant will then say the following:

"Man, do you take this Woman to be your lawfully wedded wife?"

And Man will say:

"I do."

Translation: "There's really no way for me to get out of this at this point."

And then the Manland officiant will turn to you and ask:

"And Woman, do you take this Man to be your lawfully wedded husband?"

To which you reply:

"I do."

Translation: "My dad will be so pissed if I back out of this after all the money he spent on the ceremony!"

The officiant will then tell you two to kiss and pronounce you "husband and wife." And that's pretty much it; then all of the guests jump up in the air and cheer really loud because they're happy for you. (And, more important, it's chow time!)

Congratulations! And welcome to Manland!

CHAPTER EIGHT

Living in Manland

"For my part, J travel not to go anywhere, but to go. J travel for travel's sake, the great affair is to move."
—Robert Louis Stevenson

Well, it's done. The honeymoon is over—quite literally. All your visiting family has gone back to the Motherland. The gifts have been unwrapped, mocked, and the majority of them returned. Now it is time to adjust to your new life as married Woman and Man. You think you know your Man at this point, but trust us, you don't. Married Manspeak takes on an entirely new level of sophistication and, when used against you, can result in you losing your mind.

Something like 50 percent of all Manland inductees eventually discover they are incapable of assimilating into their new surroundings and end up renouncing their citizenship and fleeing the country. The more you understand how Married Man expresses himself, the greater chance you have of beating the miserable odds stacked against Woman.

Moving into Man's Abode

Once you have established that Man is committed to you for the long run, it's safe to assume that you no longer need to stay at a hotel that charges you four hundred Manland dollars for a soda from the mini-bar. It's time to pack your suitcases, settle up your hotel bill, hand in your key, and move into his place. But there are a few ground rules you need to follow when living on Man's turf. Break these rules, and you'll be back in that stifling hotel room in no time.

1. Resist the temptation to place your box of tampons in Man's medicine chest. Feminine hygiene products frighten this creature. In theory, Man understands that you menstruate. But he really, really, really doesn't want to know when it's happening.
2. Do not put curtains on Man's windows or throw pillows on his sofa or plants on his windowsill. General rule of thumb: If it wasn't there when you arrived, don't bring it.
3. Do not listen to Man's answering machine messages while he is out. You will inevitably hear a message from someone revealing something disturbing about Man that you will wish you had never learned.
4. When it comes to home décor in Manland, it's really a matter of bargaining. You want to hang up your favorite Ansel Adams photograph? Man must be allowed to hang up his favorite Dale Earnhardt Jr. photograph. You want to display your Barbie collection in the living room? All you have to do is let Man display his collection of human bones in a glass case in the foyer.

5. Any mysterious potions, lotions, or ointments you find in Man's bathroom are not to be inquired about. Just as in the Manland military, there is a "don't ask, don't tell" policy regarding male hygiene products.

6. It is fine to introduce new clothing to Man's wardrobe, but do not discard the old. Man has an unnatural attachment to pit-stained T-shirts, poop-streaked underwear, and jeans that are either three sizes too small or three sizes too big.

7. The climate in Man's home will always be either too cold for you, or too hot. Any attempt to adjust the thermostat to a temperature that balances your homeostasis will be met with contempt. Don't tempt the fates.

Snappy Retorts

Sometimes Man has trouble prioritizing. So, when your very practical suggestion that he take you out for dinner on a special occasion is met with resistance, resist back!

Screwed-up-priorities Man says: "But the game is on tonight!"
You respond: "Then my clothes will stay on tonight!"

8. The most prized possession in Man's home . . . the thing he lives for and would kill for . . . is the television remote. The only time you will be able to get your hands

on it is when Man is either sleeping, passed out drunk, or at work. We pray, for your sake, that those moments come often.

9. Redefine your concept of a "made" bed, "clean" dishes, and "fresh" milk. Nothing is what it should be in Manland. These are no different.

10. If Man has lost something and accuses you of moving it, do not attempt to argue with him. A Man searching for a missing object cannot be reasoned with. Just sit on the sofa quietly while Man goes into panic mode, cursing and taking the Lord's name in vain as he searches high and low for the "stolen" object that, as it turns out, was right where you said it would be . . . where he left it.

Married Manspeak

Just as Man slips into subdialects when in dating mode, Man, when married, often speaks in tongues. It's understandable. Man has just signed away his life to you. He is confused by what he has done, and may, through secret code and manipulative verbal tactics, attempt to regain some of the power he feels he gave up when you were sworn in as a citizen. Understanding what Man is really saying may just give you two cuties a shot at getting to the Manland Golden Years. Probably not. But it can't hurt to dream, right?

Man says: "Anything you say, dear."
Translation: "Please shut up."

Man says: "Your girlfriend seems nice."
Translation: "Your girlfriend is so hot!"

Man says: "No, I don't think your best friend is attractive at all."

Translation: "Your friend is way hotter than you, but out of my league."

Snappy Retorts

Man is not known for his couth. So, why should you be?

Married Man says: "You've put on a few pounds."
You respond: "Yeah, boring sex does that to a woman's body."

Man says: "I'll do the dishes."

Translation: "I'll let the dog lick the dishes, then I'll put them back in the cupboard."

Man says: "I'm just gonna check the oil in the car."

Translation: "I'm just going to check the oil . . . then swap out all four tires on the car, overhaul the engine, tinker with the carburetor, replace the shock absorbers, slap on a new coat of paint, and maybe, if there's time, put leopard-skin upholstery on the seats."

Man says: "I need to go clear my mind."

Translation: "I'm going to masturbate."

Man says: "Of course I missed you!"
Translation: "You were away?"

Man says: "I love your friends."
Translation: "I love your friends . . . the ones who never come over to visit."

Man says: "Of course I used a glass."
Translation: "I had that milk carton so far down my throat you wouldn't believe."

Man says: "Wow, breast implants are becoming more and more affordable!"
Translation: "Why are your breasts so friggin' small?!"

Man says: "Hey, look! A waxing salon just opened up around the corner!"
Translation: "Man, you need a Weed Wacker to get that fuzz off your upper lip."

Man says: "Sure, honey."
Translation: "I wasn't listening to a word you just said."

Man says: "No, you're not fat."
Translation: "Yes, you are fat."

Man says: "I'm thinking."
Translation: "I'm zoning out."

Man says: "I'll remember."
Translation: "I won't remember."

Man says: "Remind me."
Translation: "Remind me, so I can still forget, but blame you for not reminding me enough."

Man says: "No, your mother did not call while you were out."
Translation: "Yes, your mother called, and I answered in a Spanish accent so she'd think she got the wrong number."

Man says: "I said I'll take the garbage out!"
Translation: "I have no intention of taking the garbage out and will leave it rotting in the house until the smell is so overwhelming you'll take it out yourself."

Man says: "I made the bed."
Translation: "I moved the pillows around."

Man says: "I can cancel poker night if you really want me to."
Translation: "I'll kill you in your sleep if you take away the one thing that keeps me sane."

Domesticating Man

When a tourist arrives at her hotel, one of the first things she does is check out her room for cleanliness. If things aren't up to par, she stomps back downstairs to the concierge and demands a new room. You have the same rights once you are a resident in Manland. You just have to fight for the rights a bit more. Man, by nature, does not see the need for domestic chores. Left to his own devices he will let mold grow on the dirty dishes, algae accumulate in the bathroom, and food rot in the refrigerator. But seeing as you do not possess Man's immunity to the many biological hazards that contaminate his country, you must disinfect your surroundings when possible. In order to train Man to place his dirty underwear in the hamper rather than leave it balled up between the sofa cushions or on the kitchen counter, you have to scare him into taking action.

By operating via a carefully devised system of actions and reactions, you can teach Man to not endanger your health.

What Man Does	*How to Stop Him*
Doesn't flush the toilet	Drop a tampon in the bowl
Leaves dirty dishes in the sink	Transfer them to his car
Leaves his dirty underwear on the couch	Refuse to take yours off at all
Puts his toenail clippings on your side of the bed	Leave yours on his side of the bed.
Tosses his wet towels on the bed	Remove his towel from the bathroom while he's in the shower.
Uses the dishrags to wipe his nose	Use his collector's edition football jerseys to wipe yours
Burps at the dinner table	Burp during sex
Uses your toothbrush to polish his shoes	Use his toothbrush to polish yours
Fails to close the cap on the shampoo bottles	Unscrew the cap on his soda bottle

Fighting Married Manspeak

Much like having your wallet stolen in South America by a bunch of armed roadside bandits working for a Colombian drug lord, fighting in Manland can cause hysteria. In order to avoid accepting blame for whatever he has done wrong, Man will manipulate and misrepresent the truth. Funny—Man will think nothing of fighting to the death with a Hell's Angel in a bar over a bowl of peanuts, or beating another Man into a raw pulp because he made a derogatory comment about Man's favorite football team. But when it comes to taking Woman on in the battle of the sexes? Well, Man is scared. He will employ any verbal tactics that can help him avoid further confrontation and extricate himself from the situation quickly. In other words, he's a chicken.

In order to level the playing field a bit when involved in a confrontation with a local, it helps to cut through Man's bull pucky.

Snappy Retorts

When Man has screwed up, he will rarely cop to it. So why should you?

Married Man says: "I swear I didn't forget our anniversary!"
You respond: "And I swear I didn't forget to tape your game."

Man says: "What did I do?"
Translation: "Oh, crap. I got caught."

Man says: "Must be your time of month."
Translation: "You're being a raving, lunatic bitch. And you do this to me every month."

Man says: "Um."
Translation: "How long is this gonna take?"

Man says: "Let it go."
Translation: "Clearly, I'm not going to win this round."

Man says: "Grrr."
Translation: "I see your point, although I do not agree with the manner in which you have chosen to express it."

Man says: (Nothing.)
Translation: "I realize that there is absolutely no way out of this, and I really don't have a clue what I even did that was so wrong, and I have absolutely no idea what you're talking about or how the hell I can get out of this, so I'm just going to stare straight ahead at the wall and pray for a self-induced coma to take over my body and get me out of this situation."

Man says: "So what!"
Translation: "I have no idea what else to say."

Man says: "Let's make up."
Translation: "Let's have sex."

Man says: "You're going to have a heart attack if you don't calm down."

Translation: "The game is coming on, so, if you could just go into the other room for a while, that would be great."

Man says: "You should have reminded me!"

Translation: "You should have reminded me four hundred times, not just three hundred ninety-nine times."

Man says: "Calm down."

Translation: "Lower your voice because everyone is staring and I'm embarrassed to be associated with you right now."

Travel Tips: *Man's Mother*

No matter how much of a wicked witch she is, never, ever bad mouth Married Man's mother. His loyalty to his creator is unflappable, and Man will never choose you over her . . . mostly because he's too afraid to.

Man says: "I have no idea what you're talking about."

Translation: "I know exactly what you're talking about, but I refuse to let you think I do because I'm hoping you'll drop the whole thing and leave me alone."

Man says: "You're nuts."

Translation: "You're nuts."

Man says: "Gee, sorry I'm not *perfect* like you!"
Translation: "Your gender is the one that ate the poison apple and doomed all of Mankind, so get over yourself already, woman!"

Man says: "I don't have to take this crap."
Translation: "I have to take this crap because I have no other place to go right now, but I'm gonna make it look like I don't have to take this crap and maybe you'll believe it and leave me alone."

Man says: "I just don't see what you're so upset about."
Translation: "I just don't see why you can't wait until the commercials to pick a fight with me."

Man says: "You're overreacting."
Translation: "If you're behaving like this now, what the hell are you going to do when you find out about the *really* bad stuff I did?"

Man says: "I'm sorry."
Translation: "I'm not sorry, but I'm saying I am because it'll shut you up."

Man says: "I swear I wasn't looking at her!"
Translation: "I was totally looking at her, but how could I help it? Her boobs were the size of cantaloupes."

Man says: "Just sit down and take a deep breath."
Translation: "You're blocking the television."

Man says: "Of course, I'm paying attention."
Translation: "I am sooooo not paying attention."

Man says: "I promise I'll do better next time."
Translation: "I'm breaking up with you tomorrow morning."

Man says: "You're just like your mother."
Translation: "You're just like Satan."

Man says: "Huh?"
Translation: "I hear you screaming something at me at the top of your lungs and see you flailing your arms around like a crazy banshee, but I can't process your statement to the fullest of my intellectual capabilities because I tuned your dolphinlike squeak out about twenty minutes ago."

Man says: "I did not!"
Translation: "I did, but I'm not copping to it."

Man says: "You know, you're not always right."
Translation: "I have yet to catch you being wrong, but one of these days . . ."

Man says: "I can't believe you're bringing that up again!"
Translation: "My god, do you ever forget *anything*?!"

Man says: "You're right. I'm wrong."
Translation: "I'm sleeping on the couch tonight, aren't I?"

Man says: "I won't do it again."
Translation: "I will absolutely do it again."

Man says: "I just don't see why you're so upset."
Translation: "I just don't see why you had to turn off the
    television to yell at me."

Well, there you have it. All the information you need to
make your way around Manland in a safe and productive manner. You've learned about Man's culture, customs, language,
mating rituals, and everything in between. Take heed of the
traveler's advice within these pages, and you will not only survive your trip to the most mysterious land of all—but you'll actually enjoy it! So, pack your bags and get on your way! Your
future awaits you—and we can't wait to see if that future is
wearing boxers or briefs.

Now, to get you in the mood for your impending journey
here is the Manland National Anthem, to be sung in the key
of . . . well, whatever.

> We're men.
> Manly men.
> We burp and fart.
> Then do it again.
>
> We have bad breath
> And hairy backs.
> We worship babes
> With perky racks.
>
> We state one thing
> But mean another
> And can't say "no"
> To our mothers.
>
> We think of sex
> And nothing more

Unless we're thinking
About the score.

We can't commit
To the female kind.
But pledge our loyalty
To beer and pork rinds.

Yes, we're men.
Manly men.
We burp and fart.
Then do it again.

Okay, so it ain't exactly poetry. But what did you expect from the gender carrying the Y chromosome?

Bon voyage!

Acknowledgments

Were it not for some special people in my life, I may very well have ended up being, not a published writer, but a toll-booth collector on the New York State Thruway. So, I'd like to declare my eternal thanks to the following people for helping me get where I am today—wherever that is:

My father and mother, Jeff and Jennifer Grambs, who perfected the art of parenting and have given me so much encouragement and inspiration. If I grow up to be half the person each of them is, I'll be a happy camper. (If not, I give them permission to put me up for adoption.) My husband, Tommy Schwing, whom I studied a great deal while researching this book. He is the wind beneath my motorcycle seat, and a true Man among men. Citadel Press, and particularly my magnificent editor, Danielle Chiotti, for making the book writing experience a complete blast, start to finish. Every writer should be so fortunate. Grace Freedson, my equally magnificent agent, who has nurtured my career with such vision, wisdom, and wit. The staff and members of the New York Friars Club—there is, quite simply, no greater place on Earth. And lastly, my incomparable circle of friends and whoever invented the Post-it.